DATE DUE	

Learning To Live From The Gospels

by

Eugenia Price

J. B. LIPPINCOTT COMPANY

PHILADELPHIA AND NEW YORK

✿ PREFACE

Learning to Live from the Gospels was written for men and women who, like myself, need to un-
learn some of the static concepts acquired from years
of religious conditioning. Men and women who need
to begin to learn, not how merely to be theologically
acceptable to their particular groups, but how to live
adequately in today's world. Perhaps it isn't a very different world, but it seems more confusing, more com-
plex. Different reactions are required from us. Old
resting places must be relinquished, old horizons
pushed up and out, if we are to function creatively
within the framework of our swiftly evolving society.
Our basic Christian absolute must remain (if we are to
keep our sanity), but the attitudes of our hearts and
the doors of our minds need to swing open to what God
is saying for *now*.

If we believe, as I most certainly do, that the written-down Word of God is as relevant today as it has always been, surely the Bible is the one source of continuing light. To "worship" the Bible *or* to debunk it is wasteful, egocentric. We need be neither bibliolaters, idolizing the written words of the Scriptures, nor swinging radicals bent on demythologizing. Both approaches feed the already outsized human ego. The balanced Christian way to learn from the Bible is to study it through our knowledge of the always contemporary person of Jesus Christ—God himself—as he is discoverable to anyone in the pages of the New Testament.

You will find little or no information here concerning who wrote and who did not write the Gospels as we know them. You will find no scientific verification for the miracles—not even a defense of them. God's activities need no defense from us. There are no scholarly apologetics, no exegeses of the more obscure passages of Scripture. I do not know how to do any of this. I find it enough to attempt to learn how to live by the passages I do understand. Having met Christ when I was well along on my earthly journey, what has held my interest from the beginning of my life with him has not been how to analyze or criticize the Bible, but *how to learn to live from it.*

My mail continues to show that people all over the world are still being confused, disturbed, shaken by some of the current Scripture debunking on which many of our learned men are spending their energies. We need to be shaken up now and then, but if faith in the eternal Christ can be destroyed by a mere book,

that faith needs to take a fresh running start anyway.
My mail also shows a growing unrest, even angry rebel-
lion at the frequently dishonest, unrealistic rigidities
of the religious legalists who fight to keep God in a box,
using the Bible to justify their dogmatism, to give
simplistic answers to the profound issues it raises.
There is room, as I see it, between those two extremes,
for people like us who have no axes to grind, but who
know we need to learn to live our ordinary daily lives
with God. Jesus was crucified by men who violently
disagreed with him, who were driven to murderous
extremes by the quiet, unshakable, revolutionary
Authority of the Son of God. Among the silk-robed
Pharisees and scribes were both the legalists and the
debunkers, but they, alone, did not crucify Jesus. We
were there, too, those of us who need to learn how to
live.

In my opinion, most of us who honestly try to understand something of what God is saying to us in the
Scriptures have never been attracted either to the rigid
rules and regulations of extreme orthodoxy or to the
abstract diffusion of radical theology. My prayer for us
all is that we will soon come to see that there is only one
absolute, one polestar—Jesus Christ, as God's own
revelation of himself. I could become lost in the quag-
mire of existentialism without the one eternal starting
place on which I can depend—the Saviour God. When
we begin with him, we are free to move ahead, sure of
our direction. Of course, we need each other. We need
the products of our shared thinking and knowledge,

but I believe we are to follow—to be truly influenced *only* by—the Christ of the Gospels.

After having worked through the Gospel accounts in the writing of this book, I am less convinced of my own ability to *understand* God, but even more convinced of the potential of every human being to *know* him. We learn how to live with a person in direct proportion to how well we know that person. God became a human being in Jesus of Nazareth for more reasons than we will ever comprehend, but one of them had to be because he *understood* us—understood that we needed to know something of what his heart is like before we could trust him fully. The man or woman who is learning to live adequately in our common, troubled world, is learning something more every day about the God with whom it is our consummate privilege to live on this earth.

I know of no better place to learn how to live than from the four provocative Gospel accounts of the earthly life of the God who loved us enough to become one of us.

EUGENIA PRICE

St. Simons Island, Georgia
May, 1968

❧ Contents

Saint Matthew

Chapter 1
vv. 21, 23

. . . thou shalt call his name JESUS: for he shall save his people from their sins. . . . they shall call his name Emmanuel, which being interpreted is, God with us.

Even in the half-light of the Old Testament period, Isaiah knew that the people needed God to be *with them*. When the prophet told of the coming of the Messiah, he said his name would be called Emmanuel—God with us. Even then, Isaiah saw the people's need to have God with them. Not remote and distant—*with them*. Surely, when the Messiah did come, he fulfilled Isaiah's prophecy and more. He was God with us, Emmanuel, but his name was called *Jesus*. And this is one of the most clarifying verses in the New Testament: right at the beginning of the first Gospel account, we are told that the Messiah's name would be called *Jesus*. God has come in Jesus, to be with us—to be Emmanuel —but our great need, as only God knew, was to be saved from our sins. Jesus means Saviour. As the New Testament completes the message of the Old, so the two names given the Messiah complete each other. God cannot freely be with a man without saving him from his sins. This is the *nature* of the redeemer God. We are saved by an always present God, because of *what he is like*—not by acceptance of a certain doctrine or the performance of a ritual.

CHAPTER 3

v. 17

> *And lo a voice from heaven, saying, This is my beloved Son, in whom I am well pleased.*

The Father was saying more than the human mind can ever comprehend when he declared that Jesus was his beloved Son, who pleased him.

One thing he must have meant was that he could *trust* his Son completely. God alone knows how trustworthy anyone is. The glory-filled moments after his baptism, when Jesus actually saw "the Spirit of God descending like a dove, and lighting upon him," must have brought an indescribable feeling of exhilaration—both human and divine. But the Father, knowing the Son as he did, knew there was in Jesus far more than feeling: There was in him complete, uncluttered trustworthiness.

CHAPTER 4

v. 1

> *Then was Jesus led up of the spirit into the wilderness to be tempted of the devil.*

Jesus did not go off into the wilderness to be tempted in order to prove his own advanced spirituality. He did not wander off alone in an ascetic daze, seeking a still more exhilarating spiritual sensation: He was "*led* up of the spirit. . . ." The Father deliberately led him into his time of conflict and agony of soul because the Father knew he could trust his Son utterly.

Jesus' temptation in the wilderness was, in a definite sense, a preliminary part of his Passion—his Cross Experience. Here, he was giving himself to us and for us just as surely as he gave himself during the bright-dark hours through which he hung on the Cross. The Father did not lead his Son into temptation to prove his trustworthiness, his inner strength, his ability to resist the tempter. The Father already knew. Jesus was led into his wilderness time for our sake. *So we would know.*

vv. 3, 6

. . . *If thou be the Son of God,* . . . . . . *If thou be the Son of God,* . . .

Until now, I have thought that the first two temptations of Jesus were peculiar to him. Twice, his very identity as the Christ was challenged: "If thou be the Son of God, . . ." "If thou be the Son of God, . . ." This seemed always to mean that only Jesus could have been tempted on this point, since only he is the divine Son of God. I now believe this is only part of it. It's true that he was challenged here in a way in which only he could have been challenged, but aren't *our identities* as forgiven, Spirit-filled sons of God challenged too by temptation? Doesn't the world look at us in the face of fresh trouble or criticism and ask: "If Christ lives in you as you claim he does, why should you go down under this thing?"

vv. 8, 9

Again, the devil taketh him up into an exceeding high mountain, and sheweth him all the kingdoms of the world, and the glory of them; And saith unto him, All these things will I give thee, if thou wilt fall down and worship me.

God does not want us to be naïve. In Jesus' wilderness experience we are told what to expect of ourselves: an overwhelming tendency to worship secularism. Christians seem to fail at this point more than at any other. Even the most doctrine-minded among us can rationalize an act if it inflates our bank accounts.

vv. 19 through 22

...Follow me, ... And they straightway left their nets, and followed him. ... and he called them. And they immediately left the ship and their father, and followed him.

Straightway. Immediately. Peter and Andrew "straightway left their nets, and followed him." James and John "immediately left the ship and their father, and followed him."

None of these men wasted time with doubt, self-analysis, cost-weighing. They didn't ask for proof that Jesus was born of a virgin or if miracles were myths. They didn't pin him down to find out whether or not he believed the Scriptures were inspired. They asked no questions about his political leanings. There was no indecision whatever. Not one of the four wrote a ten-page letter to anyone asking for advice. They simply went with him—straightway and immediately.

CHAPTER 5

vv. 1 through 12a

*And seeing the multitudes, he went up into a moun-
tain: and when he was set, his disciples came unto him:*

And he opened his mouth, and taught them, saying,

*Blessed are the poor in spirit: for theirs is the kingdom
of heaven.*

*Blessed are they that mourn: for they shall be com-
forted.*

Blessed are the meek: for they shall inherit the earth.

*Blessed are they which do hunger and thirst after
righteousness: for they shall be filled.*

Blessed are the merciful: for they shall obtain mercy.

Blessed are the pure in heart: for they shall see God.

*Blessed are the peacemakers: for they shall be called
the children of God.*

*Blessed are they which are persecuted for righteous-
ness' sake: for theirs is the kingdom of heaven.*

*Blessed are ye, when men shall revile you, and per-
secute you, and shall say all manner of evil against you
falsely, for my sake.*

Rejoice, and be exceeding glad: . . .

These verses, called the Beatitudes, sound like mad-
ness or, at best, wishful thinking to those still dwelling
in darkness. Christians have been so tormented by
failing in their foolish attempt to follow the Beatitudes
as rules laid down for living the adequate life that some
have even invented dispensations—little chopped-up
sections of time—which conveniently put the Beatitudes in another era. Any other time—but now now.
Once more, God has provided a great simplification:
If one thinks at all, it is obvious that what Jesus did

not do was lay down a list of "how-to" regulations. He was *describing* the inevitable *result* of the Spirit-filled life. *If* we have begun to permit God to live his life in us, these are the ways we will be: never proud spiritually; willing to admit our heartbreaks and our griefs— i.e., we will be realistic about life; never complaining, but rejoicing when we hunger for more righteousness— when we see our need; always merciful—willing to stand in the other person's shoes; always pure in heart— possessing unmixed motives; never relishing the role of troublemaker, willing to move out toward peace; never falling into the trap of self-pity when we have been wronged for Jesus' sake—for being a way we know it is right to be, regardless of the cost to us.

We are to rejoice and be exceeding glad when we see any of these divine family traits showing up in us in our daily round. The Beatitudes could, I suppose, be called a kind of check list—but never a set of rules. Jesus is declaring: This is the great potential for all of you.

v. 13

> *Ye are the salt of the earth: but if the salt have lost his savour, wherewith shall it be salted? it is thenceforth good for nothing, but to be cast out, and to be trodden under foot of men.*

If Christians are the salt of the earth, why do we have such a flavorless world? Jesus was not wrong. Perhaps we have just refused to realize how utterly singular— how unique—salt is. As he said: If the flavor has gone out of the salt—what is going to "salt" the salt?

v. 20

For I say unto you, That except your righteousness shall exceed the righteousness of the scribes and Pharisees, ye shall in no case enter into the kingdom of heaven.

Unless we exhibit a kind of love and understanding and wisdom that *exceeds* that demonstrated by those who are dead certain they have it all figured out, we have in no way learned the nature of the atmosphere of the Kingdom.

vv. 22, 28, 32, 34, 39, 44

But I say unto you, . . . But I say unto you, . . . But I say unto you, . . . But I say unto you, . . . But I say unto you, . . . But I say unto you, . . .

Jesus came saying (verse 18) that he was not here to discount what was tried and true of the *old*. "But *I* say unto you, . . ." We need to dwell on that often repeated phrase of his: "But I say unto you, . . ." He did not come to obliterate anything—he came bringing it all, making it all available in himself. This is what is *new:* The day for rules and regulations is past. Grace and truth have come in Jesus Christ—and with him, the whole life. *It is all in him.*

v. 45

That ye may be the children of your Father which is in heaven: for he maketh his sun to rise on the evil and on the good, and sendeth rain on the just and on the unjust.

We will know that we are the children of the Father when it begins to seem right and natural to us to *want* the sun to rise on both the evil and the good; when we *care* that the rain falls on the just and the unjust. God is love, and he loves *every man* and *every woman*—good and evil, just and unjust. This is difficult for us to accept, feeling as we do, that somehow he owes us more love because we have been driven by our own desperate need to receive his forgiveness.

v. 48

Be ye therefore perfect, even as your Father which is in heaven is perfect.

This simple statement of Jesus' has caused great frustration and confusion. People unwisely try to whip themselves up into what they consider God's perfection. This is nonsense. God is God and we are we. We are to live up to the limits of our capacities—*where we are* on our journey. We are to give out to the extent of our love—as much as we have learned about love. We are being "perfect" as the Father is perfect when we live all the love we know.

CHAPTER 6
vv. 4, 6

. . . thy Father which seeth in secret. . . . . . . thy Father which seeth in secret. . . .

The phrase ". . . thy Father which seeth in secret. . . ." is repeated three times in the first part of this chapter (also verse 18). It is *implied* many more times in what Jesus is saying. *God is a realist.* He does not bother with outward appearances, with loud, lengthy prayers, with broadcast charity. He does not bother because he does not need to bother. These are, in reality, irrelevant. "The Lord looketh on the heart." God sees motives, not performances. He sees reactions first, then actions. How much more *rest* and how much less *waste* there would be if we realized this.

vv. 14, 15

For if ye forgive men their trespasses, your heavenly Father will also forgive you: But if ye forgive not men their trespasses, neither will your Father forgive your trespasses

Jesus is not implying here that we should bargain with God; certainly not that God bargains with us. It is simply that as long as a human heart is hardened toward anyone, i.e., refusing forgiveness for any reason, it is also closed to God. He never invades. He waits for the open heart. God is always willing—eager—to forgive. But we must be in a condition to receive his forgiveness.

v. 23

. . . If therefore the light that is in thee be darkness, how great is that darkness!

Could this be at least partial explanation for the strange, often cruel personalities of men and women who profess Christ (have perhaps settled, for themselves at least, all doctrinal problems!) but whose "light" is so lacking in love, it is full of darkness?

v. 24

. . . Ye cannot serve God and mammon.

Neither can we love God and harm one of his loved ones.

v. 33

> *. . . seek ye first the kingdom of God, . . .*

If we seek God first—give him our full attention—everything else falls into place. If we are style-conscious, the designers have us. If we are money-conscious, we are owned by our bank accounts. If we are self-conscious, we insist upon self-ownership. But if we are God-conscious, the way is clear. We are off our own hands. What gets our attention gets us.

CHAPTER 7

v. 5

> *Thou hypocrite, first cast out the beam out of thine own eye; and then shalt thou see clearly to cast out the mote out of thy brother's eye.*

Not only are we blinded to how to help our brother, if we have left the "beam" in our own eye, we are also squinting and peering fuzzily at the very nature of God—unable to see him clearly either.

vv. 21 through 23

> *Not every one that saith unto me, Lord, Lord, shall enter into the kingdom of heaven; but he that doeth the will of my Father which is in heaven. Many will say to me in that day, Lord, Lord, have we not prophesied in thy name? and in thy name have cast out devils? and in thy name done many wonderful works? And then will I profess unto them, I never knew you: depart from me, ye that work iniquity.*

If "God is love," then isn't his will always centered in the inclusive necessity to love? Will only those who have dropped the art of self-defense in favor of the willingness to love enter into the Kingdom? Will he give admittance into the Kingdom for skillful expounding of the prophecies and doctrines of the Christian faith? For good deeds well done? For thrashing the devil? No. Our *Father seeth in secret,* where the heart is, where love is or isn't. And only he knows.

v. 29

For he taught them as one having authority, and not as the scribes.

Jesus was not just another writer of spiritual truths. He was God become Man, possessing both the Authority of God and the Authority of Man.

CHAPTER 8

vv. 8 through 10

The centurion answered and said, Lord, I am not worthy that thou shouldest come under my roof: but speak the word only, and my servant shall be healed. For I am a man under authority, having soldiers under me: and I say to this man, Go, and he goeth; and to another, Come, and he cometh; and to my servant, Do this, and he doeth it. When Jesus heard it, he marvelled, and said to them that followed, Verily I say unto you, I have not found so great faith, no, not in Israel.

Jesus marveled because one man understood his Authority and acted on his clear understanding. There is enormous simplification here. And great urgency for us to begin to think of how we complicate faith. We need only to recognize who God is, and begin to act on what we have recognized.

vv. 19, 20

And a certain scribe came, and said unto him, Master, I will follow thee whithersoever thou goest. And Jesus saith unto him, The foxes have holes, and the birds of the air have nests; but the Son of man hath not where to lay his head.

He made no promises of material security. If a man follows Jesus, he must not follow him for where they may be going together, but for one reason only: to be with him.

vv. 21, 22

And another of his disciples said unto him, Lord, suffer me first to go and bury my father. But Jesus said unto him, Follow me; and let the dead bury their dead.

Jesus was not being cruel here. He was simply saying: Up ahead is *life*. Follow me, and your attention will be riveted forever upon life.

CHAPTER 9

vv. 10 through 13

And it came to pass, as Jesus sat at meat in the house, behold, many publicans and sinners came and sat down with him and his disciples. And when the Pharisees saw it, they said unto his disciples, Why eateth your Master with publicans and sinners? But when Jesus heard that, he said unto them, They that be whole need not a physician, but they that are sick. But go ye and learn what that meaneth, I will have mercy, and not sacrifice: for I am not come to call the righteous, but sinners to repentance.

"Go ye and learn what that meaneth, . . ." In rebuking his critics, the shallow-thinking Pharisees, Jesus did not say, "Get out a book about love and learn what I mean." He said, *"Go ye and learn. . . ."* He knew they, who already had life decided and analyzed both intellectually and doctrinally, needed to take an *active step* in love. But he did give them one potent clue as to how to do it: "I will have mercy, and not sacrifice." The time for ceremonial sacrifices ended when the Lamb, himself, came on the scene. Spiritual arrogance cannot live in his presence.

v. 36

But when he saw the multitudes, he was moved with compassion on them, because they fainted, and were scattered abroad, as sheep having no shepherd.

If we would remember this reaction of Jesus as we read magazines and newspapers, or walk our crowded streets, we would find ourselves forgetting how to be merely shocked.

CHAPTER 10
v. 13

And if the house be worthy, let your peace come upon it: but if it be not worthy, let your peace return to you.

If we offer peace and good will in a situation and they are not received—if we are scorned, laughed at, "cut down to size" for our efforts—we have obeyed Jesus anyway. And if it has been real peace we offer, with no mixed motives, only peace can come back to us. Even if it is slammed back in our faces, we are still the recipients of peace. The same is true of love.

v. 16

Behold, I send you forth as sheep in the midst of wolves: be ye therefore wise as serpents, and harmless as doves.

Where I live there are both snakes and doves. This admonition of Jesus has taken on fresh meaning: We are to be as wise as serpents, but without their bite or venom. We are to be as harmless as doves, but without their voracious appetites or their stupidity. The dove, though beautiful, seems to be a rather stupid, uncertain bird, but surely its intentions are harmless. Otherwise it would not announce its arrival with such a whistling of its wings. The snakes in the woods around my house are silent.

vv. 19, 20

But when they deliver you up, take no thought how or what ye shall speak: for it shall be given you in that same hour what ye shall speak.

For it is not ye that speak, but the Spirit of your Father which speaketh in you.

When we are utterly frightened and helpless and at a loss for words, God's Spirit can get through to us far more easily.

v. 26

Fear them not therefore: for there is nothing covered, that shall not be revealed; and hid, that shall not be known.

One day the cover will be removed and there will stand God, obviously in full charge. And all those who cannot now believe will see him as having always been just that—God in full charge of his creation. And at that time, "... every knee shall bow."

vv. 29 through 31

Are not two sparrows sold for a farthing? and one of them shall not fall on the ground without your Father. But the very hairs of your head are all numbered. Fear ye not therefore, ye are of more value than many sparrows.

Now and then a bird flies accidentally against the screen on my back porch and breaks its neck. The Father knows. He is the only Person alive who can give full attention to every living being every minute. He is not only the only one who *can* do this; he is the only one who wants to.

vv. 34 through 37

Think not that I am come to send peace on earth: I came not to send peace, but a sword. For I am come to set a man at variance against his father, and the daughter against her mother, and the daughter in law against her mother in law. And a man's foes shall be they of his own household. He that loveth father or mother more than me is not worthy of me: and he that loveth son or daughter more than me is not worthy of me.

Jesus, of course, did not mean to imply that he had come to break up families. Invariably, he used the sharp illustration—what we now call "attention grabbers." And yet beneath this harsh-sounding statement is truth. Anyone who permits even a member of his family to cause him to drift away from Christ, from love, is heading for trouble. Jesus did not come to bring an easy peace. He came to bring *lasting* peace. Every form of indulgent sentimentality must be cut away before anyone can follow the Christ of Calvary. But when indulgent sentimentality is gone, *love* can replace it.

CHAPTER 11

vv. 2, 3

> *Now when John had heard in the prison the works of Christ, he sent two of his disciples, and said unto him, Art thou he that should come, or do we look for another?*

John the Baptist was a God-centered man of enormous faith. And yet, when Jesus did nothing to bring about John's release from prison, but went out teaching and preaching, John—quite understandably—began to doubt. Plainly, he began to doubt that Jesus was the One he, John, had been heralding for so long. John, by the standard of human accomplishment, was the greatest religious leader of his time. Jesus said of him: (verse 11) ". . . Among them that are born of women there hath not risen a greater than John the Baptist: . . ." Still, here was this great prophet of God *doubting* the very heart of the message God had given him to preach to the people. If John, the messenger of God, harbored doubts, how ridiculous that *we* are surprised, shocked when we also doubt! Are we greater than John? Do we have more spiritual depth? More spiritual perception? These are irrelevant questions. The relevant question is: Do we have the *humility* of John? *Authentic humility can afford to admit doubt.* John made no attempt to hide his uncertainty. He sent two of his own disciples to Jesus to ask him point-blank—two men who had followed John for all the days he had gone about preaching. Even before his followers, John's humility stood up. He cared more about discovering the truth, having his doubts put down, than he cared about his own reputation as a religious leader. To doubt is not necessarily un-Christian. To lack humility *is*.

vv. 4, 5

Jesus answered and said unto them, Go and shew John again those things which ye do hear and see: The blind receive their sight, and the lame walk, the lepers are cleansed, and the deaf hear, the dead are raised up, and the poor have the gospel preached to them.

In answer to John's question, Jesus said simply that the disciples of John were to tell the Baptist what they had seen there: The blind were seeing again, the lame were walking, the lepers were being healed, the deaf heard, the dead lived and the good news was being given to those who so desperately needed it. He did not send John's two friends back to their teacher in prison with a carefully set forth theological treatise. He sent them with one fact: Creativity is taking place! Nothing is being torn down that has stood from the beginning. Everything is only being strengthened, made new, restored.

v. 6

And blessed is he, whosoever shall not be offended in me.

Jesus sent word to John entirely sufficient to end John's doubt, but being Jesus, he went a step farther. Jesus did not admonish John in this statement; he encouraged him. To me, it was as though Jesus were saying *more* than "Yes, John, I am the One who fits, according to your message, into the divine plan." He was also saying, "I supersede even the divine plan! Even in prison, John, you will find peace if you do not lose your faith in *me*. Not merely in my mission on earth, but in *me*."

v. 11

Verily I say unto you, Among them that are born of women there hath not risen a greater than John the Baptist: notwithstanding he that is least in the kingdom of heaven is greater than he.

Jesus praised John the Baptist. He went so far as to declare there had never been a man born of woman who was greater. *But,* and this is the key: As great as John was, the most insignificant person who is *born into* the Kingdom would be greater! This in no way denigrates John. Rather, it clarifies Jesus' set of values: the very values of God himself. No one was more loyal than John, no one more sacrificial, no one expended his energies more recklessly. But these, valuable as they are, are not the qualifications for entering the Kingdom of God. There is but one: faith in Jesus Christ.

v. 12

And from the days of John the Baptist until now the
kingdom of heaven suffereth violence, and the violent
take it by force.

This is a difficult passage. I have never been entirely
satisfied with the explanations I have read concerning
it. The words "violence" and "force" have been distorted for us by current news coverage. So, perhaps a
look at a newer translation is needed. J. B. Phillips
translates verse 12 this way: "From the days of John
the Baptist until now, the Kingdom of Heaven has been
taken by storm and eager men are forcing their way into
it." The Amplified: "And from the days of John the
Baptist until the present time the kingdom of heaven
has endured violent assault, and violent men seize it by
force [as a precious prize]—a share in the heavenly
kingdom is sought for with most ardent zeal and intense
exertion." Other versions give similar light. At this
point in my own thinking, I believe that at least part
of what Jesus was saying had to do with the sudden
availability of the Kingdom to the common man. Until
John the Baptist, the people had to depend upon their
priests. The holy of holies was closed to them. Suddenly, it was no longer closed. And they plunged into
God's presence. How have we so diminished the wonder
of the open door that men no longer attempt to rush
into the Kingdom of God?

vv. 16 through 19

But whereunto shall I liken this generation? It is like
unto children sitting in the markets, and calling unto

their fellows, and saying, we have piped unto you, and ye have not danced; we have mourned unto you, and ye have not lamented. For John came neither eating nor drinking, and they say, He hath a devil. The Son of man came eating and drinking, and they say, Behold a man gluttonous and a winebibber, a friend of publicans and sinners. But wisdom is justified of her children.

Jesus' irony here is, as always, more than attractive, it is profound. He is saying in a highly colorful manner that there is no pleasing the public! The immaturity of the masses of people sticks out all over: If you don't dance when I play my pipes or mourn when I want to play funeral, I won't play. The same irony permeates the sharp comparison he made between himself and John the Baptist. He said in effect: "John was bred to austerity, to the lonely life, to the aesthetic way, and you said he had a devil. I come being utterly and warmly and joyfully human, 'eating and drinking' and enjoying myself and enjoying you. So, you tack a label on me. I'm a glutton and I'm a winebibber. There is no satisfying the public. But wisdom—the wisdom of God available to anyone who will take it—is justified, is proven only by her actions. You're all talking too much!"

vv. 25, 26

At that time Jesus answered and said, I thank thee, O Father, Lord of heaven and earth, because thou hast hid these things from the wise and prudent, and hast revealed them unto babes. Even so, Father: for so it seemed good in thy sight.

Jesus had just finishel upbraiding the sinfulness and materialism and immorality of cities where he had attempted to make his purpose clear. They would be far less fortunate in the judgment than the wicked, ancient cities of Tyre and Sidon—even Sodom. Jesus Christ had not come to them, but the people of Chorazin and Bethsaida and Capernaum *had been exposed to him,* had seen his love in operation, had heard his message. They had had a chance—firsthand—to see their need of repentance.

And immediately following this caustic statement, it is as though he sighed, reminding even himself—with thanksgiving—that the Father had dared to be clear and simple. Had not settled for revealing himself to the "wise and prudent"—the scholarly intellectuals—but had made himself clear in such a way that even children could grasp his identity. There is no indication anywhere in the Bible that we need to be brilliant or clever or learned in order to know God. There is every indication that all of us, even the brilliant and the clever and the learned, *must be childlike.* This was "good" in the Father's sight because only the unsuspicious, open heart, with no false confidence in itself, *can trust.* The Father is always realistic about both things and people.

vv. 28 through 30

Come unto me, all ye that labour and are heavy laden, and I will give you rest. Take my yoke upon you, and learn of me; for I am meek and lowly in heart: and ye shall find rest unto your souls. For my yoke is easy, and my burden is light.

Jesus' strong warning to Chorazin and Bethsaida and Capernaum (vv. 20 through 24) is followed by his strongest claim to the Authority of God (v. 27). But here, he differs from so many of his well-meaning servants who settle for ending with a tirade against the sinfulness of man: Jesus never settled merely for convicting a man of his sin; he always offered freedom, rest, peace. "Come unto me, all ye that labour and are heavy laden, and I will give you rest." When he blazed out at sinfulness, he did not direct his fire at the sinner. They received the full force of his love! Condemnation cannot bring rest. Guilt cannot bring rest. Jesus was never about the business of causing anxiety. He was about his Father's business, and this was to bring sinful man back into the restful, creative relationship of Eden.

Anxious, restless Christians are a contradiction of the Gospel of Christ. "Because of who I am," he declared, "I will rest you—if you will only come to me and give me a chance." As always, he took the time and expended the effort to explain—if an explanation was really necessary. The idea of rest in the deeps of the human spirit in the midst of any trouble required explanation and he made it. "Take my yoke upon you, and learn of me. . . ." We have read at length about the fact that Jesus understood the value of yokes, that he made them with his own hands in Joseph's carpenter shop. But too often, we stop with the yoke. He did not. In the very same sentence, he gave us the most important instruction even he ever gave: ". . . *learn of me*. . . ." Discover for yourselves, he told us, something of the true nature of this God who longs over you. Find out what he is really like in his heart, his plans, his dreams for the people he loves. Don't settle for a secondhand notion of God. Learn of him firsthand by learning of Jesus Christ, his one complete, uncluttered, clear revelation of himself. Rest comes no other way. Through Christ, it can come to everyone. With him, no one is left out.

CHAPTER 12
v. 7

 . . . I will have mercy, and not sacrifice, . . .

For all the years until Jesus came clarifying God, man had depended upon his own ability to make a suitable sacrifice. It is clear now, if we will only see, that mercy outshines any sacrifice we could imagine. God would rather see us showing mercy than writing large checks.

v. 13

 Then saith he to the man, Stretch forth thine hand. And he stretched it forth; and it was restored whole, like as the other.

God does not require nor want our sacrifices. The supreme sacrifice has already been made on Calvary. But there is a part for us. God is not interested in mere manipulation of the human heart. Jesus healed the man with the withered hand, but the man had to "stretch forth (his) hand." The healing became useful to him when he had done his human part. God always desires *our* participation.

v. 19

He shall not strive, nor cry; neither shall any man hear his voice in the streets.

Jesus did not come making a display of himself, shouting at the top of his lungs; he did not walk the earth blowing trumpets or setting up high-pressure organizations for purposes of newspaper coverage or promotion. He sent out no four-color brochures, no flyers for store windows. He did not thump a pulpit nor cry into a microphone. "He shall not strive, nor cry; neither shall any man hear his voice in the streets." He worked sanely, quietly, profoundly, with the dignity of love. Notice specifically that he did not "strive." His work was exhausting, constant, but his inner peace held. Jesus was crucified on a Cross. He did not drop dead from striving to do in his human strength what only the supernatural God could do.

vv. 31, 32

Wherefore I say unto you, All manner of sin and blasphemy shall be forgiven unto men: but the blasphemy against the Holy Ghost shall not be forgiven unto men. And whosoever speaketh a word against the Son of man, it shall be forgiven him: but whosoever speaketh against the Holy Ghost, it shall not be forgiven him, neither in this world, neither in the world to come.

In my opinion, these two verses have caused more unnecessary heartache and inner misery than any other in the entire Bible. Surely, I do not know all their meaning. But Jesus Christ never caused unnecessary confusion. He still does not. God is *never* "the author of confusion."

At least once a month I receive one or more letters from some trembling, anxious person who is sure he or she has committed the unpardonable sin against the Holy Spirit. Stop and think: If a human heart cares enough one way or the other to be distraught with worry and concern over a thing like this, doesn't it make sense that that person could not possibly have committed such a sin? In the first place, one has to *believe* in the Holy Spirit before one cares at all about sinning against him! Doesn't the very question answer itself? Do you fear you have committed the unpardonable sin against the Holy Spirit? I don't think I understand all of what that sin might be, but if you are worried about it, you certainly have not!

vv. 46 through 50

While he yet talked to the people, behold, his mother and his brethren stood without, desiring to speak with him. Then one said unto him, Behold, thy mother and thy brethren stand without, desiring to speak with thee. But he answered and said unto him that told him, Who is my mother? and who are my brethren? And he stretched forth his hand toward his disciples, and said, Behold my mother and my brethren! For whosoever shall do the will of my Father which is in heaven, the same is my brother, and sister, and mother.

Jesus was not *excluding* his mother or his brothers. He was *including* us.

CHAPTER 13

vv. 54 through 58

And when he was come into his own country, he taught them in their synagogue, insomuch that they were astonished, and said, Whence hath this man this wisdom, and these mighty works? Is not this the carpenter's son? is not his mother called Mary? and his brethren, James, and Joses, and Simon, and Judas? And his sisters, are they not all with us? Whence then hath this man all these things? And they were offended in him. But Jesus said unto them, A prophet is not without honour, save in his own country, and in his own house. And he did not many mighty works there because of their unbelief.

Jesus' visit to his home town was not publicized. He came home quietly, being himself. He hadn't maneuvered any honorary degrees, nor bought any time on any communications media. He just came home the way he left, *being* the Son of God, *being himself.* The home-town folk were not impressed. They knew his mother and father as their neighbors. They knew all Jesus' brothers and sisters by name. They had no more faith in him than in any other home-town young man. As a consequence, he "did not many mighty works there because of their unbelief."

In this startling sense, we *do* control the "mighty works" of God!

CHAPTER 14

vv. 10 through 14

And he sent, and beheaded John in the prison. And his head was brought in a charger, and given to the damsel: and she brought it to her mother. And his disciples came, and took up the body, and buried it, and went and told Jesus. When Jesus heard of it, he departed thence by ship into a desert place apart: and when the people had heard thereof, they followed him on foot out of the cities. And Jesus went forth, and saw a great multitude, and was moved with compassion toward them, and he healed their sick.

Jesus loved John the Baptist. They were not only cousins; they had been united in the purpose of God. They shared the same goals. We are not told in detail of their personal relationship, but there can be little doubt that the two were close, or that John's ignominious death grieved Jesus. He tried to get away alone in order to cope with his loss. It was impossible to get away. The crowds followed him, and the sight of their crippled legs and blind eyes and empty souls caused his compassion to overcome his grief. He did what he had to do: He showed them his heart.

v. 27

. . . Be of good cheer; it is I; be not afraid.

After Jesus had fed the multitudes toward whom he had shown compassion, he sent his disciples away in a ship and dismissed the people—still longing, needing to be alone with the Father. By evening, he had managed some time for himself, for healing of his grief, for new strength. But his disciples were out on the sea in their small ship when a storm began to whip up gigantic waves, tossing their boat dangerously. "He was there alone," but he was also God, and he knew his men were afraid without him. Once more, he relinquished his much needed solitude and ". . . went unto them, walking on the sea." Of course, the disciples were terrified. To their minds, the sight of a man coming toward their plunging boat across the black fury of the stormy water, had to be a spirit—an apparition! They ". . . cried out for fear." And then Jesus said a most important, many-dimensioned thing: "Be of good cheer!" he called out to them. "It is I; be not afraid."

I have always been struck by the fact that he said "Cheer up" first. He is still calling out to us when the wind turns our normally quiet waters into a whirlpool of fury that can suck us under or batter us to our knees in abject fear. I have known his call to change entire lives. As I write this, at a time that could bring me fear, I hear his call to me: "Cheer up! Don't be afraid—it is I!"

He is in every blast of trouble, every moment of panic, every time of pressure, of fear, of grief, of confusion. And he is not an apparition—this call to us from the very heart of God is not a mere phrase to stiffen our spines—it is reality. "It is I." *He is in it.* And where he is, fear vanishes and the courage of good cheer returns.

vv. 32, 33

> *And when they were come into the ship, the wind ceased. Then they that were in the ship came and worshipped him, saying, Of a truth thou art the Son of God.*

When Jesus and poor human Peter climbed aboard the tossing ship, "the wind ceased." And the disciples said: "Of a truth thou art the Son of God." There is no better way to be certain of that than to have had him sweep one's fear away.

CHAPTER 15
v. 14

Let them alone: they be blind leaders of the blind. And if the blind lead the blind, both shall fall into the ditch.

Good advice. When one is struck full in the face by Pharisaism, don't complain, don't attack, don't try to change them—let them alone.

CHAPTER 16
vv. 11, 12

How is it that ye do not understand that I spake it not to you concerning bread, that ye should beware of the leaven of the Pharisees and of the Sadducees? Then understood they how that he bade them not beware of the leaven of bread, but of the doctrine of the Pharisees and of the Sadducees.

We should not wonder at the wild array of fringe cults among people who seek God. Without the teaching of Jesus, made clear to us (as he promised) through his Holy Spirit, it is no wonder at all that men become confused. Look at the very men who lived and slept and ate and worked with Jesus when he was on earth! Read these verses with the idea of seeing how "far out" they were much of the time in their understanding.

Jesus said, "Take heed, and beware the leaven of the Pharisees and of the Sudducees." The disciples, their

minds on the fact that they forgot to bring any bread
along, missed his point entirely. Shaking his head, perhaps, he asked them if they had forgotten so soon that
he had fed—not only the five thousand when there was
no food, but a short time later—seven thousand. His
reminder that it would be utterly ridiculous for him
to worry about forgotten bread when he had himself
made bread for thousands finally cleared their muddled
minds a little. And they saw that he was warning them
about "doctrine clutchers." Not the leaven of bread—
the leaven of the hypocritical spirit. This leaven grows
inside a man's heart in no time. It flatters his ego to
feel himself right above all men. It is tempting.

vv. 13 through 18

*When Jesus came into the coast of Caesarea Phi-
lippi, he asked his disciples, saying, Whom do men say
that I the Son of man am? And they said, Some say that
thou art John the Baptist: some, Elias; and others,
Jeremias, or one of the prophets. He saith unto them,
But whom say ye that I am? And Simon Peter answered
and said, Thou art the Christ, the Son of the Living God.
And Jesus answered and said unto him, Blessed art thou,
Simon Bar-jona: for flesh and blood hath not revealed it
unto thee, but my Father which is in heaven. And I say
also unto thee, That thou art Peter, and upon this rock
I will build my church; and the gates of hell shall not
prevail against it.*

Although I have written many times on Peter's
sudden declaration that Jesus was the Christ, the Son
of God, I confess some uncertainty as to the sequence
of realization among Jesus' disciples. We have just noted

in Matthew's Chapter 14, verse 33, that when Jesus got into the boat with them and the wind subsided, *they* called him the Son of God. And yet, Peter said: "Thou art the *Christ,* the Son of the living God." There is little doubt that this was the first time anyone had experienced and voiced the *entire truth* about his identity. The dawn of full truth broke slowly and gradually upon the men and women who followed him during the years of his earthly life. Even though the men in the boat—his close, intimate associates—declared him to be the Son of God, the use of the name *Christ* meant that Peter knew the Messiah had come! The fact that when, on the sandy coastal road at Caesarea Philippi, Jesus asked: "Whom do men say that I am?" showed that he, Jesus, was well aware of the confusion in men's minds. The fact that his own disciples mentioned that people were hinting that he was John the Baptist returned from the dead, or Elijah or Jeremiah, indicates the talk going around. Talk, full of questionings and theories. Peter nailed it down for all time, and Jesus blessed him and assured him that this all important flash of truth came straight from the Father. There had apparently been no gossip that he was the Messiah. No man had told Peter. The Father was able to get through to Peter and Jesus said, "Blessed art thou, Simon Bar-jona. . . ." And Jesus, because Peter had grasped this central truth, the rock beneath all other truth, changed Simon's name to Peter, which meant "rock." Peter had, by the grace of God, set his feet on the Rock—the fact that Jesus of Nazareth *was* the

Christ, the Son of the living God. On this Rock—this truth and this truth alone—did Jesus feel safe in building his church.

vv. 21 through 23

From that time forth began Jesus to shew unto his disciples, how that he must go unto Jerusalem, and suffer many things of the elders and chief priests and scribes, and be killed, and be raised again the third day. Then Peter took him, and began to rebuke him, saying, Be it far from thee, Lord: this shall not be unto thee. But he turned, and said unto Peter, Get thee behind me, Satan: thou art an offence unto me: for thou savourest not the things that be of God, but those that be of men.

Here the first dark cloud appeared in the exhilarating, clear sky of the men who followed Jesus. Immediately after Peter declared him to be the Christ, the Son of the living God, Jesus began to tell them of the tragedy ahead. He made sure, first, that they knew his true identity, and then he spoke of his planned journey to Jerusalem, his suffering and betrayal, his death and resurrection. It seems doubtful that they heard the word "resurrection," so stunned were they that he was going to walk knowingly into his death. At least Peter rebuked him and told him nothing like that should ever happen to *his* Master. Here again, Peter was being his old impulsive self. He had just uttered the truth central to all human fulfillment, and in a matter of minutes, he was on his own again, saying a foolish thing. So foolish, so beside the point, that Jesus called the same man he had just blessed and complimented, "Satan!" Now, of course, he was not calling Peter names. He was, as always, speaking truth. ". . . thou savourest not the things that be of God, but those that be of men." Peter was impatient for a materialistic, earthly kingdom in which he would have a prominent place. Just another reason why Jesus would not have planned to build his church on Peter, a mere man. On any man.

vv. 24 through 28

Then said Jesus unto his disciples, If any man will come after me, let him deny himself, and take up his cross, and follow me. For whosoever will save his life shall lose it: and whosoever will lose his life for my sake shall find it. For what is a man profited, if he shall gain the whole world, and lose his own soul? or what shall a man give in exchange for his soul? For the Son of man shall come in the glory of his Father with his angels; and then he shall reward every man according to his works. Verily I say unto you, There be some standing here, which shall not taste of death, till they see the Son of man coming in his kingdom.

From here on, the sky grows darker, the sayings harder—not only to hear, but to understand. Talk from the Master of self-denial, of each man taking up his own cross. Talk that smacked only of defeat and failure. Even when he spoke of himself as coming "in the glory of his Father with his angels" to reward them for their good works, his meaning must have fallen flat around them. Talk of his impending death had frightened and discouraged them, had stultified their minds. They felt anxious and uncertain about their own future. They had learned to love him as both Master and Man— intimate Companion, Leader—what would life be without him? Their own anxious hearts and confused minds blinded and deafened them to what he was saying. They were deaf to what he said about his own Cross and about the crosses they were to take up for his sake. Verse 28. "Verily I say unto you. There be some standing here, which shall not taste of death, till they see the Son of man coming in his kingdom." How this must have confused them! Wasn't he already there? Did he mean *not* to set up his kingdom right there in their land *for them*? How many interpretations have you read of this strange verse? As many as I have, no doubt, but is it wrong to think that this was true? That most of the men standing there in the road at Caesarea Philippi with Jesus that day did not taste death until he came in his kingdom? Judas tasted death by his own hand, but didn't the King come back in his own Kingdom *at Pentecost*? It's worth thinking through.

CHAPTER 17

v. 3

And, behold, there appeared unto them Moses and Elias talking with him.

One provocative thought about the appearance of Moses and Elijah on the mountain when Jesus was transfigured before his three disciples, Peter, James and John: In spite of their utterly human frailties, *he saw their potential.* These three men were the ones he trusted to *see* him transfigured. They were the three he felt he could trust (once his Spirit indwelt them) with having experienced this brilliant sight.

And just now, I am struck for the first time with the *nearness,* the proximity of those who have left this earth in physical death and have begun living in the Eternal: *In a moment,* Elijah and Moses were there, recognizable as Elijah and Moses!

Those who are out of our sight here are not far away. They are close.

v. 5

   . . . This is my beloved Son, . . .

Once more, the Father speaks of his son. How he loved him! How pleased he was with him. "This is my beloved Son, in whom I am well pleased." The same words he spoke about Jesus at his baptism in the beginning of his earthly ministry. Now, near the end, the words again: "This is my beloved Son, in whom I am well pleased." Did the Father say this to him on the Cross? More. He did more then than speak words to his beloved Son. *He held him.* And loved us through him as he hung there.

CHAPTER 18
v. 1

   At the same time came the disciples unto Jesus, saying, Who is the greatest in the kingdom of heaven?

Peter, James and John had just come down from their high spiritual experience on the Mount of Transfiguration and joined right in with the others to ask: "Who is the greatest in the kingdom of heaven?"

Well, Pentecost had not happened yet. Visions and high moments are not enough to keep us spiritually sane or humble.

v. 11

For the Son of man is come to save that which was lost.

Pity those who think he came for any other reason.

vv. 12, 13

How think ye? if a man have an hundred sheep, and one of them be gone astray, doth he not leave the ninety and nine, and goeth into the mountains, and seeketh that which is gone astray? And if so be that he find it, verily I say unto you, he rejoiceth more of that sheep, than of the ninety and nine which went not astray.

Does this mean Jesus is more pleased to have us go astray and return than to have us remain loyal to him? Ridiculous thought. And yet, early in my own Christian life, when I was wound up like a tight spring and speaking of nothing except *my* conversion, *my* forgiveness for the sin in *my* life, some mixed-up souls asked me this question. God is simply extra joyful to see one of his loved ones saved from self-destruction, and he can't help rejoicing. The ninety and nine had caused him no anguish. The *one* did. Even God rejoices when he is relieved of anguish. Either way, God loves everyone.

vv. 19, 20

Again I say unto you, That if two of you shall agree on earth as touching any thing that they shall ask, it shall be done for them of my Father which is in heaven. For where two or three are gathered together in my name, there am I in the midst of them.

This is not merely a prayer technique. It is a fact.

CHAPTER 19
vv. 23, 24, 26

Then said Jesus unto his disciples, Verily I say unto you, That a rich man shall hardly enter into the kingdom of heaven. And again I say unto you, It is easier for a camel to go through the eye of a needle, than for a rich man to enter into the kingdom of God. . . . but with God all things are possible.

Jesus had nothing against rich men. God has nothing against rich men now. It is simply true that God is a realist. He and he alone knows how hard a thing is for a man to do in that man's particular circumstance.

v. 30

But many that are first shall be last; and the last shall be first.

We're going to be very, very surprised one day.

CHAPTER 20
vv. 15, 16

Is it not lawful for me to do what I will with mine own? Is thine eye evil, because I am good? So the last shall be first, and the first last: for many be called, but few chosen.

God has rights. And he alone merits them. He knows. This is why judgment was put into the hands of Jesus Christ. And God's judgment and God's justice can never, never be measured by what *we understand* of judgment or justice. For this I am grateful.

vv. 17, 18, 19

And Jesus going up to Jerusalem took the twelve disciples apart in the way, and said unto them, Behold, we go up to Jerusalem; and the Son of man shall be betrayed unto the chief priests and unto the scribes, and they shall condemn him to death, And shall deliver him to the Gentiles to mock, and to scourge, and to crucify him and the third day he shall rise again.

The sky darkens still more. They are on their way to Jerusalem. For the second time he tries to make them understand that he will die and rise again. His patience is unbelievable, *until* we know him better.

vv. 20, 21

Then came to him the mother of Zebedee's children with her sons, worshipping him, and desiring a certain thing of him. And he said unto her, What wilt thou? She saith unto him, Grant that these my two sons may sit, the one on thy right hand, and the other on the left, in thy kingdom.

For the second time he has told them of what lies ahead. He will be scourged, he will be betrayed, he will be murdered. And almost at once the mother of Zebedee's children, James and John, pops her impudent question: She wants *her* two boys in the choice seats in Christ's earthly kingdom. Evidently no one was listening to him. As too many of us do not listen. We, like Zebedee's wife, Jesus' relative, are too preoccupied with our own ambitions.

CHAPTER 21

v. 10

And when he was come into Jerusalem, all the city was moved, saying, Who is this?

When Jesus comes on the scene, people are *moved,* And always there is the question: Who is he? "Who is this?" His identity goes on being the key.

v. 15

. . . and the children crying in the temple, and saying, Hosanna to the son of David; . . .

The children knew who he was.

v. 22

And all things, whatsoever ye shall ask in prayer, believing, ye shall receive.

Neither is this a prayer technique. It is also a fact.

v. 23

. . . By what authority doest thou these things? And who gave thee this authority?

His identity again. "By what authority . . . ?" Until one knows *who he is,* understanding is not possible. Faith is *less* possible.

CHAPTER 22

v. 15

Then went the Pharisees, and took counsel how they might entangle him in his talk.

Sound familiar? He was not entanglable!

v. 34

> *But when the Pharisees had heard that he had put the Sadducees to silence, they were gathered together.*

The Pharisees were so pleased that he had silenced their rivals, the Sadducees, they ". . . gathered together." They had a committee meeting and tried new tactics.

CHAPTER 23

v. 3 (Read vv. 1 through 10.)

> *All therefore whatsoever they bid you observe, that observe and do; but do not ye after their works: for they say, and do not.*

This is an astounding passage when it is read thoughtfully. Jesus instructed his disciples to conform—that is, not to be known as renegade rebels. And yet, in the plainest of language, he warned them not to imitate the *attitudes* of those scribes and Pharisees in charge of their formal worship! "They are sayers and not doers," he declared. "They will load you with burdensome rules and laws and not move a finger to help you bear them!" They (the scribes and Pharisees—you know them today) are people-pleasers, "spiritual" exhibitionists, showoffs. They love the best rooms, the front seats in church. They revel in being called Rabbi, Rabbi—or as we might say today—leader. "But don't yearn to be known as a leader," he admonished them. There is only one leader—Christ. Just as there is only one Father in heaven.

Much of this may seem contradictory. He is urging

us to go along with those who "sit in Moses' seat"; that is, go to church, join the fellowship, obey those who lay down the rules, but do not *be* like them! Shun *being as they are.* How few of us dare to suspect that our Lord was willing to trust us to such difficult extents. To suggest that such delicate balance would be possible among mere mortals. But he did. And it is, because he indwells us now. *Pentecost has happened.* We can be guided by his very mind within us.

vv. 11 through 13, 37

> *But he that is great among you shall be your servant. And whosoever shall exalt himself shall be abased; and he that shall humble himself shall be exalted. But woe unto you, scribes and Pharisees, hypocrites! for ye shut up the kingdom of heaven against men: for ye neither go in yourselves, neither suffer ye them that are entering to go in. . . . O Jerusalem, Jerusalem, thou that killest the prophets and stonest them which are sent unto thee, how often would I have gathered thy children together, even as a hen gathereth her chickens under her wings, and ye would not!*

Be courteous and obey the rules of your church, even if among the deacons or officials of that church, *you know* for a fact that there are "scribes and Pharisees." But remember, *they* are not the greatest in the kingdom of God, no matter how important their committee appointments. They love their positions and their robes of authority, but "he that is greatest among you shall be your servant. And whosoever shall exalt himself shall be abased; and he that shall humble himself shall be exalted." The glorious, relieving paradox of God!

Note: If possible, read this entire chapter carefully in *several* modern translations, particularly *Good News for Modern Man* (American Bible Society).

"But woe unto you, scribes and Pharisees, hypocrites!" I know of no other place where Jesus spoke at such length, or with such severity *against* anything. He did not launch into thoughtless tirades. He spoke with reason and logic, and his teaching is always more thought-provoking than emotion-arousing. This blast is not an emotion-arouser, either. It is hard fact about the attitude of heart which obviously is the most repugnant to God! The attitude of heart which is at the opposite pole from what God intended. The pharasaical heart, the hypocritical heart is anathema to God. Twice, Jesus showed anger, fury at what he saw on earth— here, in this scathing denouncement and when he drove the money-changers from the Temple. Both outbursts hit at the same evil—hypocrisy. He did not blaze away at Mary Magdalene or Judas, he blazed at the Pharisees, the "impostors" in the Kingdom of God. *But* for a redemptive reason: *Everything he did and everything he said always led directly toward the potential of redemption.* In verse 37, he demonstrated the Father heart, the attitude of God toward everyone, including the hypocrites, by a shattering outburst of compassion toward the city where the scribes and Pharisees and Sadducees ruled: "O Jerusalem, Jerusalem, . . . how often would I have gathered thy children together, even as a hen gathereth her chickens under her wings, and ye would not!"

He condoned nothing that was not holy, but his heart, his God-heart, could not close toward anyone, even the "impostors" in the Holy City.

CHAPTER 24
vv. 34 through 36

Verily I say unto you, This generation shall not pass, till all these things be fulfilled. Heaven and earth shall pass away, but my words shall not pass away. But of that day and hour knoweth no man, no, not the angels of heaven, but my Father only.

This chapter is an enigma to me. There are scholars and nonscholars who write entire books on it. I would not dare try. In verse 34, Jesus said: "This generation shall not pass, till all these things be fulfilled." Was he wrong about the end? The consummation of life on earth? Some authorities believe he was. At least one school of scholarship contends that this is one "proof" that Jesus was merely a human being who *achieved* the closest of all relationships with the Father through faith and obedience. I am not swayed by this. Neither am I swayed by those who "specialize" in the Second Coming—even by those who "wait" for it and, with every new generation, find the "definite signs" which convince them that the end is near. Jesus said his "words shall not pass away" and he also said that all judgment had been placed in his hands by the Father. This is enough for me. I can trust his judgment concerning the end of things, just as I can trust his love to redeem and keep me. He also said, ". . . of that day and hour knoweth no man, . . ." But the Father does know, and this is more than enough. We can trust him with all of it. After all, he is "the beginning and the end." Whatever God does will be right and fair and creative. If I have trusted him with the beginning, I can trust him with the end.

CHAPTER 25

vv. 34 through 40

Then shall the King say unto them on his right hand, Come, ye blessed of my Father, inherit the kingdom prepared for you from the foundation of the world: For I was an hungred, and ye gave me meat: I was thirsty, and ye gave me drink: I was a stranger, and ye took me in: Naked, and ye clothed me: I was sick, and ye visited me: I was in prison, and ye came unto me. Then shall the righteous answer him, saying, Lord, when saw we thee an hungred, and fed thee? or thirsty, and gave thee drink? When saw we thee a stranger, and took thee in? or naked, and clothed thee? Or when saw we thee sick, or in prison, and came unto thee? And the King shall answer and say unto them, Verily I say unto you, Inasmuch as ye have done it unto one of the least of these my brethren, ye have done it unto me.

I feel the same about this chapter. The only part of it in which we have control are these verses. We can learn from them something—enough, surely—of the key to God's judgment of us. We are to *love,* and to show our love in concrete ways. The rest we can leave in his hands. Either we trust him or we don't. Beware of the trap of having to decide with our minds about what God has planned.

CHAPTER 26

vv. 3 through 5

> *Then assembled together the chief priests, and the scribes, and the elders of the people, unto the palace of the high priest, who was called Caiaphas, And consulted that they might take Jesus by subtilty, and kill him. But they said, Not on the feast day, lest there be an uproar among the people.*

Doesn't this sound familiar? The religious "authorities" who "have it all figured" get together to decide how to "cut their man down to size" by *subtlety*. "Let's not do anything rash," they insist. "Nothing that will bring criticism to our own fine spirituality and prestige. Let's get rid of him, by all means, but in a subtle, careful way so it will appear that *he* and not *we* are in the wrong. We will be clever and let him hang himself! Not on our feast day, mind you, because this would cause the people to rise up against *us*."

I have been gotten rid of "by subtlety." Perhaps so have you. I know of at least a dozen of my close friends who have also been given the "subtle" treatment just before they were put out of their "religious" jobs or their "religious" organizations, were even pushed out of their churches. God tells us, in effect: "Don't be surprised that this happens to you. It also happened to me. Part of the reason I permitted it to happen to me is so you would be able to identify with me when your time comes and so that you would know that I also know how you feel!"

v. 11 (Read vv. 6 through13.)

For ye have the poor always with you; but me ye have not always.

Jesus is not here saying that nothing matters but the spiritual. He is not suggesting that we are to ignore the poor because they are always with us. He is saying something far deeper: Love comes first. Love of God, as he really is, will bear the kind of fruit that takes care of the human needs of man. He is showing us here that there is a right sequence: Love God and then we will automatically love man.

v. 25

Then Judas, which betrayed him, answered and said, Master, is it I? He said unto him, Thou hast said.

Jesus did not say "Yes" when Judas asked: "Is it I?" He did not need to. He knew that Judas knew. There is a clue here to the ridiculousness of some of our prayers when we pray: "Lord, *if* I have sinned, forgive me." He created right into us an antenna that picks up our sin for us. We know about our sin, *if* we are living near the Source of all goodness.

vv. 31, 32

Then saith Jesus unto them, All ye shall be offended because of me this night: for it is written, I will smite the shepherd, and the sheep of the flock shall be scattered abroad. But after I am risen again, I will go before you into Galilee.

He gave them ample warning of the trouble ahead. He also gave them ample confidence: "But after I am risen again, I will go before you into Galilee." He would meet them at their familiar place, where they would be at home again with him. Safe. As with all he said, there is a dimension here for us, too. We all have trouble up ahead. No one is immune to the sudden shock, the quick tragedy, the bitter failure. At those times it seems almost certain that God is dead for us. He and his disciples lived out the drama—the familiar drama that has always haunted man. Trouble strikes, God seems dead, and then, if we trust him, he always, by some means, sees us through it. He is risen now forever. As I write this, I am living through a trouble spot *knowing,* reckoning on the fact that he has gone before me into *my* Galilee, where things will somehow be right again. The problem may not be solved, but he will be there waiting for me. That is always enough.

vv. 33 through 35

> *Peter answered and said unto him, Though all men shall be offended because of thee, yet will I never be offended. Jesus said unto him, Verily I say unto thee, That this night, before the cock crow, thou shalt deny me thrice. Peter said unto him, Though I should die with thee, yet will I not deny thee. Likewise also said all the disciples.*

I have just now noticed that the incident of Peter's boasting claim to eternal loyalty follows the passage in which Jesus promised to be there waiting for them after their trouble struck. This, too, is for us. It is glib of us,

as it was glib and superficial of Peter, to insist that we
know how we are going to react in any circumstance.
Jesus knew what Peter would do before the cock crowed
the third time. He knows what we will do. This knowing does not change his love. He will still be there
up ahead, in our Galilee waiting for us.

vv. 38, 40

Then saith he unto them, My soul is exceeding sor-
rowful, even unto death: tarry ye here, and watch with
me. . . . What, could ye not watch with me one hour?

Little should be said here. Much should be thought,
taken in, absorbed, allowed to become a part of us, as
our very breath is a part of us. Jesus Christ, the Son of
God, *needed* his friends.

vv. 43 through 45

And he came and found them asleep again: for their
eyes were heavy. And he left them, and went away again,
and prayed the third time, saying the same words. Then
cometh he to his disciples, and saith unto them, Sleep on
now, and take your rest: behold, the hour is at hand,
and the Son of man is betrayed into the hands of sinners.

The men kept falling asleep when he needed them
to be with him. For a moment, his humanity took over,
as he came back to where they slept, almost begging
them to wake up and help him. When they did not, he
settled it alone with his Father, the only way anyone
can really settle anything. It is human to run to our
friends. Jesus did. He does not condemn us for this,

but waits for us to do as he did, go finally to the Father alone and transact business on the ground of his love. Jesus' suffering was still up ahead, but once he had done this, he could walk again to where the disciples slept and tell them to go on and get their rest. His heart had grown quiet in the ugly face of what lay just ahead.

vv. 48, 49

Now he that betrayed him gave them a sign, saying, Whomsoever I shall kiss, that same is he: hold him fast. And forthwith he came to Jesus, and said, Hail, master; and kissed him.

Judas is pictured as the essence of evil. People hate him, consider his sin the supreme sin. I wonder. I don't know, but I wonder. It has always seemed to me that at least we should think on the possibility that Judas was driven by impatience and ambition. Could it be that, like some of us, he thought he could coerce his Master into plunging ahead to establish that kingdom on earth so that he, Judas, could take his place in it as a valued minister? Aren't there men and women who follow Christ, as Judas followed him, believing that by deciding *for* God, they will reap their reward? And when it does not turn out that way, as it did not for Judas, they turn against God in deed or at least in reaction?

vv. 63 through 65

But Jesus held his peace. And the high priest answered and said unto him, I adjure thee by the living God, that thou tell us whether thou be the Christ, the Son of God. Jesus saith unto him, Thou hast said: nevertheless I say unto you, Hereafter shall ye see the Son of man sitting on the right hand of power, and coming in the clouds of heaven. Then the high priest rent his clothes, saying, He hath spoken blasphemy; what further need have we of witnesses? behold, now ye have heard his blasphemy.

Even against the array of false witnesses, *Jesus held his peace.* He "considered the source" and found it unworthy of self-defense. How much injury we would avoid if we could only learn the value of considering the source of our injury.

The high priest dared him to say he was the Christ, the Son of God. He said even more, and immediately there went up the cry of "blasphemy." What Jesus said went directly against what they had staked their success upon. They *had to be right,* and when he proved them wrong, he had to be a blasphemer. In just one more deliberate way, he walked into their trap for our sakes. If he had not, we could not believe in him. He was considering us then as he is considering us now.

v. 75

And Peter remembered the word of Jesus, which said unto him, Before the cock crow, thou shalt deny me thrice. And he went out, and wept bitterly.

No wonder Peter wept. He had just gotten the first clear look at himself as he really was. I believe Peter honestly thought he would not deny Jesus, no matter what happened. He was not consciously bluffing. He just didn't know himself. Like many of us, he had to learn the hard way.

CHAPTER 27

v. 2

And when they had bound him, they led him away, and delivered him to Pontius Pilate the governor.

How ridiculous and self-revealing of them to bind him! He had offered not one gesture of resistance. His persecutors were being driven to extremes by the very strutting sin which he was about to blot out on his Cross. For them too, it was blotted out. Love can go no further than he went.

vv. 3 through 5

Then Judas, which had betrayed him, when he saw that he was condemned, repented himself, and brought again the thirty pieces of silver to the chief priests and elders. Saying, I have sinned in that I have betrayed the innocent blood. And they said, What is that to us? see thou to that. And he cast down the pieces of silver in the temple, and departed, and went and hanged himself.

Judas repented, but he repented in the presence of the helpless priests and elders—helpless to *forgive* him. He had managed things his own way and by that very management had shut himself off from the presence of the only One who could have forgiven him. We have no way of knowing that Jesus did not hear his repentance; he "heard" many things that were not even spoken, and perhaps Judas was forgiven. He would be forgiven if he repented, even after what he did, or my whole concept of God's forgiveness is wrong. But Judas had maneuvered Jesus' arrest. If the Master forgave him, Judas was too far away to hear. Jesus was bound and being led away to Pontius Pilate. And not knowing, Judas threw away the thirty pieces of hated silver and killed himself.

v. 19

When he was set down on the judgment seat, his wife sent unto him, saying, Have thou nothing to do with that just man: for I have suffered many things this day in a dream because of him.

New light into the *limitless reaches of God's love* is shown me in that, through his wife's dream, God was giving even Pilate a chance to act on the truth he was hearing straight from the lips of the Son of God. Pilate listened to the people instead.

v. 25

Then answered all the people, and said, His blood be on us, and on our children.

We wonder at the frenzy, the uncontrolled anger and outright stupidity of mob action. We say we can't understand how demonstrations can turn to riots, how men and women whipped into rage can burn buildings and throw stones and snipe from rooftops with rifles. It's all here, in its wildest, most destructive form. We have not changed.

vv. 28 through 30

And they stripped him, and put on him a scarlet robe. And when they had platted a crown of thorns, they put it upon his head, and a reed in his right hand: and they bowed the knee before him, and mocked him, saying, Hail, King of the Jews! And they spit upon him, and took the reed, and smote him on the head.

The violence and injustice poured upon him—even the spitting and the jeering—paled alongside his inner certainty. Selfish, sinful men go wild in the presence of holiness. Holiness stood, unmoved, unstained in their midst.

vv. 45, 46

Now from the sixth hour there was darkness over all the land unto the ninth hour. And about the ninth hour Jesus cried with a loud voice, saying, Eli, Eli, lama sabachthani? that is to say, My God, my God, why hast thou forsaken me?

Darkness fell over the land because man was trying to put out the only true Light forever. And, as he hung on his Cross, because he was human as well as divine, there came—even for Jesus—one lightless moment: The total realization of the full load of mankind's sin so crowded his heart that he felt cut off from the Father, and cried: "My God, My God, why hast thou forsaken me?" He did not cry: "*Hast* thou forsaken me?" *He felt forsaken*. His consciousness that the Father was with him, sustaining him, had held him through the Garden of Gethsemane, the betrayal, the mock trials, the scourgings, the humiliation, the desertion by his disciples, the first hours of agony on the Cross. But there came that moment, when he was unable not to cry *with a loud voice;* unable not to ask *why*. We have no record to my knowledge that Jesus had ever asked *why* of the Father before. He had asked that if it be possible, he might avoid the Cross. But he did not ask *why* his Father had not thought of another way to show us his redemptive love. No one knows fully the reason for his cry in that one black moment. But surely, we can receive some help in our own moments of agony when our loud cries push up through broken hearts to form themselves into that same helpless word: Why? If Jesus went this far in order to make identification with me in my sufferings, in order to let me know that he knows how I feel, some of my own pain drops away. At least, a light breaks into my darkness. A ray of light for me straight from his black moment on the Cross.

vv. 57 through 61

When the even was come, there came a rich man of Arimathæa, named Joseph, who also himself was Jesus' disciple: He went to Pilate, and begged the body of Jesus. Then Pilate commanded the body to be delivered. And when Joseph had taken the body, he wrapped it in a clean linen cloth. And laid it in his own new tomb, which he had hewn out in the rock: and he rolled a great stone to the door of the sepulchre, and departed. And there was Mary Magdalene, and the other Mary, sitting over against the sepulchre.

Not until now do we have any record that the rich man, Joseph of Arimathea, had taken any public step to show that he was a disciple of Jesus. Perhaps he had only then come to believe in him. At any rate, he did what he could do because of his influence and his wealth. He was powerful enough to gain an audience with Pilate and to persuade him to give him the body of his dead Master. He was wealthy enough to have his own fine sepulchre ready. We are told that Joseph himself took the body and wrapped it in clean linen and laid it in his own sepulchre. But then he went away. The women who had loved Jesus for so long and had ministered to his needs up and down the dusty roads of Galilee and Judea did not leave. They could not. At the end, when Joseph of Arimathea had walked away, two of these women were still there, sitting beside the sepulchre and one of them was Mary Magdalene.

v. 66

So they went, and made the sepulchre sure, sealing the stone, and setting a watch.

How ludicrous that they imagined a mere stone could keep him inside. He, who had created the stone itself.

CHAPTER 28

vv. 1 through 7

In the end of the sabbath, as it began to dawn toward the first day of the week, came Mary Magdalene and the other Mary to see the sepulchre. And, behold, there was a great earthquake: for the angel of the Lord descended from heaven, and came and rolled back the stone from the door, and sat upon it. His countenance was like lightning, and his raiment white as snow: And for fear of him the keepers did shake, and became as dead men. And the angel answered and said unto the women, Fear not ye: for I know that ye seek Jesus, which was crucified. He is not here: for he is risen, as he said. Come,

*see the place where the Lord lay. And go quickly, and
tell his disciples that he is risen from the dead; and, behold, he goeth before you into Galilee; there shall ye see
him: lo, I have told you.*

Their grief must have been so mingled with the
horror they had experienced watching him die on the
Cross that much of what he had said to them was erased
from their memories. Each time he had told them he
would be crucified, he had also told them he would
rise again. Shock and tragedy do this to us. Still, early
on the first day of the week at dawn, the two Marys were
there. At least they would be near his mutilated body,
even though the big sepulchre stone separated them.
According to Matthew, the angel did not come to roll
the stone away until the women arrived. Everything
God does is done *for people,* never only to display his
power to an empty universe. It is beyond me to imagine
the new shock and the new kind of joy and wonder that
must have flooded these women's hearts as the angel of
the Lord told them their beloved Master had risen as
he said he would. And, oh, we must *never* miss God's
marvelous continuity: The angel of the Lord used the
very same words Jesus had used with them when he
said he would *go before them into Galilee* and meet
them there. Not only is God the master of perfect continuity, he never fails to make his promises accessible
to us. Have you ever noticed that the promises of God
in the Scriptures are always plain and understandable?
The difficult portions seldom contain promises. *His
promises are clear.* He knows we have trouble under-

standing when we are grieved, or ill, or weary, or defeated. The angel spoke in *Jesus' own words* to the Marys as they stood beside the open, empty tomb that first Easter morning. They were to go quickly and tell the men, his closest friends, who had deserted him in his need. God, in the face of their weakness, made sure he sent the women to let the fainthearted men know that he *had* risen as he said. ". . . Go quickly, and tell his disciples. . . ." They had run away, but he wanted them to know, too. He wanted their faith restored.

vv. 9, 10

And as they went to tell his disciples, behold, Jesus met them, saying, All hail. And they came and held him by the feet, and worshipped him. Then said Jesus unto them, Be not afraid: go tell my brethren that they go into Galilee, and there shall they see me.

And as the women ran to tell, Jesus himself met them. The risen Lord, giving them his own triumphant greeting. The Williams translation says he called: "Good morning!" The Emphasized New Testament translates the King James' "All Hail!" as "Joy to you!" Somewhere I have read one footnote that translated it: "Oh, joy!" J. B. Phillips interprets it as "Peace be with you!" I like them all. Whatever his actual words, they had to be words of joy, the very joy of God that now, it *was* all finished! The way back into the Garden of Eden was open forever to all people who would come home. And as the women fell to their knees, holding his feet and worshiping him in their great joy, he reminded them once more that they were to go tell his frightened brothers that he would be waiting for them all in Galilee.

v. 20

Teaching them to observe all things whatsoever I have commanded you: and, lo, I am with you alway, even unto the end of the world. Amen.

Back in Galilee together, *with some of the brothers still doubting,* Jesus went right on and made the statement that should be enough for us all forever: ". . . lo, I am with you alway, even unto the end of the world." In *Discoveries,* the first book I ever wrote, I recently came upon this line: "I find that as long as I am aware of his presence, I am adequate for any event." I had known him less than two years when I wrote it. Now, almost twenty years later, it is still true. As long as we are aware that God has said he will never leave us, we are adequate to anything.

Saint Mark

Chapter 1
vv. 12 through 14

And immediately the spirit driveth him into the wilderness. And he was there in the wilderness forty days, tempted of Satan; and was with the wild beasts; and the angels ministered unto him. Now after that John was put in prison, Jesus came into Galilee, preaching the gospel of the kingdom of God, . . .

In two short verses (12, 13) Mark covers the temptation in the wilderness. And no one can say it is not covered. The word "immediately" moves us from the baptism to the temptation. Mark sees no need for detail. If Jesus (verse 14) went directly from the wilderness experience into Galilee, "preaching the gospel of the kingdom of God," obviously he had overcome his tempter!

v. 22

And they were astonished at his doctrine: for he taught them as one that had authority, and not as the scribes.

The word "astonished" sets the tone for his entire ministry. Mark himself seems astonished. We should be, too.

vv. 30, 31

But Simon's wife's mother lay sick of a fever, and anon they tell him of her. And he came and took her by the hand, and lifted her up; and immediately the fever left her, and she ministered unto them.

When Jesus raised Simon's mother-in-law from her sickbed, he did more than heal her body. He healed her to begin ministering to those around her.

v. 33

And all the city was gathered together at the door.

What better way to describe the magnetism of Christ? Simon's mother-in-law was not a famous woman. Neither was Simon. But Jesus was there!

v. 45

But he went out, and began to publish it much, and to blaze abroad the matter, insomuch that Jesus could no more openly enter into the city, but was without in desert places: and they came to him from every quarter.

Here is an instance of Mark's interesting choice of words. When Jesus had healed the leper and charged him not to tell anyone so that his ministry could go on without the constant deterrent of more and more crowds, Mark writes: "But he went out, and began to publish it much, and to blaze abroad the matter. . . ." Jesus needed to cover a wider territory, to expose more and more people to himself. His compassion was not in short supply, but his time was. Still, the man *blazed abroad* the news of his healing and "they came to him from every quarter." Jesus did not wander leisurely about the countryside robed in spotless garments, raising his hand in slow, studied gestures, speaking only gentle words. He was *besieged* by the crowds because his fame began to be blazed abroad. His was the most active of lives, the roughest in many respects, the most strenuous. And much of his energy was spent in trying to dodge the multitudes in order to get away alone to pray for strength and wisdom. In the other three Gospel accounts, there is less indication of this tightly packed, pressure-filled schedule. We need to be aware of it. Mark makes certain we are.

CHAPTER 2
vv. 5, 7

When Jesus saw their faith, he said unto the sick of the palsy, Son, thy sins be forgiven thee. . . . Why doth this man thus speak blasphemies? who can forgive sins but God only?

Back in Capernaum, it is once more noised around that Jesus is there and the crowds grew so large that four friends, unable to get in, tore a hole in the roof of the house and lowered their palsied friend at Jesus' feet. Here, we see him moving toward the central reason for his coming to earth: He forgave the sick man of his sins! Jesus did not come primarily to heal sick bodies and open blind eyes and deaf ears. *He came to save people from their sins.* Of course, when he mentioned this his real trouble began. To show the relationship between the spiritual and the physical, he healed the man, also. But first, he forgave him of his sins.

vv. 13, 14

And he went forth again by the sea side; and all the multitude resorted unto him, and he taught them. And as he passed by, he saw Levi the son of Alphæus sitting at the receipt of custom, and said unto him, Follow me. And he arose and followed him.

I like Levi. Looking from the viewpoint of the average churchgoer, Levi would be the last man on earth Christ would call to become one of his intimate disciples. He was a publican, a tax collector—money-hungry, materialistic, expedient—a real worldling. Jesus knew this, and so he saw to it that, when Levi first glimpsed him, he was being followed by a multitude. This would impress Levi! Jesus loved him, wanted him, and so he called him in the one way Levi could understand. Jesus knew he could change the man once they were living together.

vv. 16, 18

. . . How is it that he eateth and drinketh with publicans and sinners? . . . Why do the disciples of John and of the Pharisees fast, but thy disciples fast not?

Here Mark begins his account of the succession of tricky questions thrown at Jesus morning, noon and night. The Master's wit and brilliant mind fairly crackle in these verses. But seldom, if ever, did he resort only to humor or satire. "They that are whole hath no need of a physician, but they that are sick. . . ." That much is humor, genuine wit. But he did not stop there: ". . . I came not to call the righteous, but sinners to repentance."

When they attempted to trick him on the question of fasting, reminding him that John's disciples fasted and his did not (inferring a piety in the disciples of John the Baptist and a lack of it among his), he answered with a humorous remark about a bridegroom's presence with the "children of the bridechamber." Then, a profound thrust broke into his humor: "But the days will come, when the bridegroom shall be taken away from them, and then shall they fast. . . ." While he was with them, while they were all together and working, Jesus believed utterly in joy and good times. Time enough when they took him away for sadness and fasting.

CHAPTER 3

vv. 1 through 5

And he entered again into the synagogue; and there was a man there which had a withered hand. And they watched him, whether he would heal him on the sabbath day; that they might accuse him. And he saith unto the man which had the withered hand, Stand forth. And he saith unto them, Is it lawful to do good on the sabbath days, or to do evil? to save life, or to kill? But they held their peace. And when he had looked round about on them with anger, being grieved for the hardness of their hearts, he saith unto the man, Stretch forth thine hand. And he stretched it out: and his hand was restored whole as the other.

Here, Jesus is turning the tables on his questioners. And he does it dramatically, commanding the man with the withered hand to, "Stand up and come out here in front!" (Phillips). Then Jesus turned to the hecklers and asked the question (verse 4): "Is it lawful to do good on the sabbath days, or to do evil? To save life, or to kill?" When they refused to answer, it angered and hurt him. He was not angered by their stubbornness, rather by the hardness of their hearts. He then asked the crippled man to stretch out his hand, and when he did, it was made whole. Never did Christ separate his truth from his love. He healed as he taught and he taught as he healed.

v. 6

And the Pharisees went forth, and straightway took counsel with the Herodians against him, how they might destroy him.

In one quick sentence Mark begins the movement toward the Cross. "Straightway," when they saw Jesus heal a man on the Sabbath, they began to make their plans to get rid of him.

Chapter 4

v. 41

And they feared exceedingly, and said one to another, What manner of man is this, that even the wind and the sea obey him?

When Jesus had quieted the storm, perhaps for the first time his disciples began to realize that their Master was different from all other teachers on earth. Up to now, it is quite possible they followed his attractive human personality, reveled in his wit, his keen perception, were captivated by the type of pungent, astute wisdom reported in the first part of Chapter 4. Now, "they feared exceedingly, and said one to another, What manner of man is this, that even the wind and the sea obey him?"

CHAPTER 5

v. 6

But when he saw Jesus afar off, he ran and worshipped him, . . .

Even this demented, tormented, animal-like man found, down deep in his twisted being, a response to the Son of God.

vv. 15, 17

And they come to Jesus, and see him that was possessed with the devil, and had the legion, sitting, and clothed, and in his right mind: and they were afraid. . . . And they began to pray him to depart out of their coasts.

The people had become so accustomed to the wild machinations of the insane Gadarene, they were more afraid of him when Jesus returned him to his right mind than they had been before!

This was too much for them. Too much goodness and power let loose. "And they began to pray him [Jesus] to depart out of their coasts."

vv. 18 through 20

And when he was come into the ship, he that had been possessed with the devil prayed him that he might be with him. Howbeit Jesus suffered him not, but saith unto him, Go home to thy friends, and tell them how great things the Lord hath done for thee, and hath had compassion on thee. And he dparted, and began to publish in

Decapolis how great things Jesus had done for him: and all men did marvel.

This is a most interesting point. Up to now, Jesus had asked those he healed not to tell. When the grateful Gadarene begged to go with Jesus, Jesus refused him, but told *him* to go "tell them how great things the Lord hath done for thee, and hath had compassion on thee." He does not trust us according to our abilities or our education or our connections with the right people. He trusts us with his work according to what he knows he has been permitted to do for us.

Evidently, according to verse 20, the Gadarene did a good job for him.

vv. 27, 28

When she had heard of Jesus, came in the press behind, and touched his garment. For she said, If I may touch but his clothes, I shall be whole.

We do not have to beg God to take some action toward us. This woman touched him and he had not even seen her until he looked around for her. If we have learned something of his true nature, have formed the habit of knowing there is healing in his very person, we can often just reach out and receive what we need. His gifts are always ready to our hand.

Chapter 6

vv. 1, 2, 3

And he went out from thence, and came into his own country; and his disciples follow him. And when the sabbath day was come, he began to teach in the syna-

gogue: and many hearing him were astonished, saying, From whence hath this man these things? and what wisdom is this which is given unto him, that even such mighty works are wrought by his hands? Is not this the carpenter, the son of Mary, the brother of James, and Joses, and of Juda, and Simon? and are not his sisters here with us? And they were offended at him.

Back in his own home town of Nazareth, instead of pride in his great works and his marvelous teaching, his old friends and neighbors "were offended at him." Evidently even the members of his immediate family were not with him, either, because he said: "No prophet goes unhonored—except in his native town or with his own relations or in his own home!" (verse 4, Phillips). This is true, and just as too much adulation from strangers can smother, lack of caring and faith from our loved ones can wound us.

v. 14

And king Herod heard of him; (for his name was spread abroad:) and he said, That John the Baptist was risen from the dead, and therefore mighty works do shew forth themselves in him.

Poor old Herod, still guilty over having been talked into killing John the Baptist, doubtless felt every good man or prophet *could* be John coming back to haunt him!

v. 42

And they did all eat, and were filled.

Everyone always is when God does the providing. "He will fill the hungry with good things."

v. 56

> *. . . as many as touched him were made whole.*

As many as touch him will always be made whole.
But we are not to sit back idly and wait. We are to
exercise our wills and *touch him.*

CHAPTER 7

vv. 6 through 9

> *He answered and said unto them, Well hath Esaias
> prophesied of you hypocrites, as it is written, This people
> honoureth me with their lips, but their heart is far from
> me. Howbeit in vain do they worship me, teaching for
> doctrines the commandments of men. For laying aside
> the commandment of God, ye hold the tradition of men,
> as the washing of pots and cups: and many other such
> like things ye do. And he said unto them, Full well ye
> reject the commandment of God, that ye may keep your
> own tradition.*

God is far less interested in what we say and do than
in what *we are.* He is not impressed with traditionalists,
yet he is not against tradition; rather he is *for origi-
nality:* newness of spirit.

v. 13

> *Making the word of God of none effect through
> your tradition, . . .*

Man is to worship the living God, not tradition.

vv. 15 through 23

> *There is nothing from without a man, that entering
> into him can defile him: but the things which come out
> of him, those are they that defile the man. If any man*

*have ears to hear, let him hear. And when he was
entered into the house from the people, his disciples
asked him concerning the parable. And he saith unto
them, Are ye so without understanding also? Do ye not
perceive, that whatsoever thing from without entereth
into the man, it cannot defile him; Because it entereth
not into his heart, but into the belly, and goeth out into
the draught, purging all meats? And he said, That which
cometh out of the man, that defileth the man. For from
within, out of the heart of men, proceed evil thoughts,
adulteries, fornications, murders, Thefts, covetousness,
wickedness, deceit, lasciviousness, an evil eye, blasphemy,
pride, foolishness: All these evil things come from
within, and defile the man.*

Read these verses carefully. How has it happened that
so many sincere, well-meaning Christians have reversed
this? Have so reversed what Jesus said that in some
Christian schools and organizations a pledge not to do
this or that or the other must be signed before a student
can matriculate or an employee be hired? Doesn't it
seem a dangerous thing to reverse the order of God?

CHAPTER 8

vv. 3, 8, 9

*And if I send them away fasting to their own houses,
they will faint by the way: for divers of them came from
far. . . . So they did eat, and were filled: and they took
up of the broken meat that was left seven baskets. And
they that had eaten were about four thousand: and he
sent them away.*

He was not only interested in his crowds as long as
they were listening to him, (as long as the "meeting"

was in progress). He was concerned about them on the
way home too.

vv. 34, 35

> *And when he had called the people unto him with his
> disciples also, he said unto them, Whosoever will come
> after me, let him deny himself, and take up his cross,
> and follow me. For whosoever will save his life shall lose
> it; but whosoever shall lose his life for my sake and the
> gospel's, the same shall save it.*

Two things come to me here. Jesus, who usually had
trouble avoiding crowds, *this time,* because of the importance of what he was about to say, "called the people
unto him with his disciples also, . . ." Could it be that
he was attempting to show the disciples (his close twelve)
that what he had to say to them was not theirs exclusively? Could it be, too, that because this is one of
his most difficult teachings, he was putting them on
their mettle—before outsiders? His reason is not important, I suppose, but it is interesting that he called
the people for this particular message and did not keep
it exclusively for his immediate helpers. One other
point: The twelve must have been shocked by what he
said. After all, they believed they had been following
him all along! Now, he was saying they, along with
everyone else, had to pick up a cross in order to follow
him. That they had to lose their lives in order to save
them. The twelve had been following Jesus, sure that
their doing so would give them a special spot in his
kingdom. They loved him humanly speaking, but he

was their key to success too. And here he is saying there is only self-denial up ahead.

vv. 2 (Read through v. 8.)

And after six days Jesus taketh with him Peter, and James, and John, and leadeth them up into an high mountain apart by themselves: and he was transfigured before them.

So much is here in these seven verses. First of all, Peter and James and John must have been stunned by the sudden transfiguration of their familiar Master. His ordinary clothing became more radiant and dazzling than any earthly bleaching could have made it. And then, before their eyes appeared Elijah and Moses, who began a direct conversation with Jesus. We do not know that the three disciples understood the conversation. They were undoubtedly too appalled by what they saw. Peter was so beside himself with awe and fright, he "really did not know what to say" (Phillips). But, being Peter, he had to say something and so in the midst of the supernatural conversation, he blurted: "Master, it is wonderful for us to be here! Shall we put up three shelters—one for you, one for Moses and one for Elijah?" (Phillips). Then God handled their confusion for them: ". . . there was a cloud that overshadowed them: and a voice came out of the cloud, saying, This is my beloved Son: hear him."

Was God saying that the day of Elijah and Moses had

passed? Important as it had been, was it now (for purposes of the spiritual life of man) history? Surely, he pointed them directly to his Son and commanded that they "hear *him*." And my favorite part of the incident: ". . . suddenly, when they had looked round about, they saw no man any more, save Jesus only with themselves."

Peter was going to build houses for everybody. God said no. *Look at my Son only.*

How is it that so many serious students of the Bible fall into the trap of controversy concerning events in the Old Testament when the Lord of the Scriptures has made this whole thing so clear in Jesus Christ? What we don't understand we can put aside and look only at Jesus.

vv. 20 through 24

And they brought him unto him: and when he saw him, straightway the spirit tare him; and he fell on the ground, and wallowed foaming. And he asked his father, How long is it ago since this came unto him? And he said, Of a child. And ofttimes it hath cast him into the fire, and into the waters, to destroy him: but if thou canst do any thing, have compassion on us, and help us. Jesus said unto him, If thou canst believe, all things are possible to him that believeth. And straightway the father of the child cried out, and said with tears, Lord, I believe; help thou mine unbelief.

Jesus here made a definite effort to involve the sick child's father, too. First, he asked a question about the child's history. Then he told the man that the child could be well again if he, the parent, believed it. "And straightway the father of the child cried out, and said with tears, Lord, I believe; help thou mine unbelief."

More than once I have been thankful that this verse is in the New Testament. The man believed just enough to trust Christ to help him believe fully. I am in this predicament often. We all are, if we admit it. And there is rest and strength and an opening for more faith just in the saying: "Lord, I believe—help thou mine unbelief!"

vv. 38 through 40

And John answered him, saying, Master, we saw one casting out devils in thy name, and he followeth not us: and we forbad him, because he followeth not us. But Jesus said, Forbid him not: for there is no man which shall do a miracle in my name, that can lightly speak evil of me. For he that is not against us is on our part.

When one looks around at various smug religious groups, one can only wonder if those people have read these verses. The disciples were smug in their position as his followers. *They* lived and traveled with him. What right did an outsider have to cast out demons in the name of *their* Master? Jesus set them straight. At least he tried. We are to *include,* never *exclude.*

CHAPTER 10

v. 17 (Read through v. 24.)

And when he was gone forth into the way, there came one running, and kneeled to him, and asked him, Good Master, what shall I do that I may inherit eternal life?

Jesus knew, the minute the rich young man came asking his question, what the outcome would be. It once seemed to me that Jesus was splitting hairs when he admonished the young man not to call him "good." Now, I see He knew the boy would try flattery first—anything to manage the answer he hoped for. Anything to cause the Master to forget to tell him he would have to let go of his money god. Jesus knew he would not win the rich young ruler, but he must have shared with his disciples later how he felt about the boy: He loved him. He wanted him as a follower, but not on the young man's terms. Only God's terms work. Another thing I see now is that Jesus did not high-pressure him. He permitted the saddened young man to walk away. Until he could put his trust in God and not in his riches, there was no point in detaining him.

vv. 25 through 27

It is easier for a camel to go through the eye of a needle, than for a rich man to enter into the kingdom of God. And they were astonished out of measure, saying among themselves. Who then can be saved? And Jesus looking upon them saith, With men it is impossible, but not with God: for with God all things are possible.

No man can talk a rich man out of his faith in his riches into faith in God. But God can do even this! ". . . I, if I be lifted up . . . , will draw *all* men unto me" (John 12:32).

vv. 28 through 30

Then Peter began to say unto him, Lo we have left all, and have followed thee. And Jesus answered and said,

Verily I say unto you, There is no man that hath left house, or brethren, or sisters, or father, or mother, or wife, or children, or lands, for my sake, and the gospel's, But he shall receive an hundredfold now in this time, houses, and brethren, and sisters, and mothers, and children, and lands, with persecutions; and in the world to come eternal life.

Too often we feel that everything Jesus said to his disciples was hard. Peter reminded the Master that they had left all to follow him. Jesus agreed and told them their reward would be great. The disciples seemed so slow to learn, every word of commendation from him must have been worth all the riches in the world to them. There was one thorn in his commendation, though, his promise of riches: He said they would receive "an hundred fold now in this time, houses, and brethren and sisters, and mothers, and children, and lands, *with persecutions;* and in the world to come eternal life." There is always the cost of discipleship, but it is not always material poverty. Few of God's true disciples are ever for long in real material want. Success is not promised, nor is material wealth promised, but the normal mind indwelt by the Spirit of God is a balanced, adequate mind—adequate to earn a living and adequate to suffer want and persecutions. Adequate to live life as it really is.

v. 32 (Read through v. 45.)

And they were in the way going up to Jerusalem; and Jesus went before them: and they were amazed; and as they followed, they were afraid. And he took again the twelve, and began to tell them what things should happen unto him.

Read verses 32 through 34 carefully. He is giving the disciples a detailed description of what is ahead for him. As they walk toward Jerusalem, they are not walking in ignorance of what to expect. He knows the agony in store for him, even to the humiliating detail of the spitting. Then read verse 35: John, the "beloved disciple," and his brother James seemed to let all the Master said run off like water off a duck's back! He is telling them of his sufferings to come and they ask if he will do for *them* right then whatever they ask of him. Both men wanted choice seats in his "glory." The day their Master mounted the throne of the earthly kingdom they still believed he would set up, these two wanted to be on his left and his right. It seems not only crass, insensitive, but totally selfish. Only Jesus knows exactly what their motives were. Perhaps their motives, like many of ours, were mixed. Perhaps they wanted to sit in those places to be near him—perhaps. At any rate, he did not scold them. He used their self-centered request, as he always did, to teach them all.

CHAPTER 11
vv. 8 through 10.

And many spread their garments in the way: and others cut down branches off the trees, and strawed them in the way. And they that went before, and they that followed, cried, saying, Hosanna; Blessed is he that cometh in the name of the Lord: Blessed be the kingdom of our

father David, that cometh in the name of the Lord:
Hosanna in the highest.

The crowds were strewing his path with branches
and shouting "Hosanna in the highest!" But I doubt
that he was fooled. I think of him riding along on his
little colt, almost unaware of the empty adulation. He
knew it was empty. In a few days some of the same
celebrants would be shouting "Crucify him!"

v. 25

And when ye stand praying, forgive, if ye have ought
against any: that your Father also which is in heaven
may forgive you your trespasses.

Here again, this is not just another "prayer technique." When "we stand praying" we know when our
prayers are amiss. And remember, only when we forgive those who trespass against us do our hearts open
to the forgiveness of God.

vv. 27 through 33

And they come again to Jerusalem: and as he was
walking in the temple, there come to him the chief
priests, and the scribes, and the elders, And say unto
him, By what authority doest thou these things? and who
gave thee this authority to do these things? And Jesus
answered and said unto them, I will also ask of you one
question, and answer me, and I will tell you by what
authority I do these things. The baptism of John, was it
from heaven, or of men? answer me. And they reasoned
with themselves, saying, If we shall say, From heaven; he
will say, Why then did ye not believe him? But if we
shall say, Of men; they feared the people: for all men

counted John, that he was a prophet indeed. And they answered and said unto Jesus, We cannot tell. And Jesus answering saith unto them, Neither do I tell you by what authority I do these things.

The old scribes and the chief priests and the elders, his faithful hecklers, were after him once more, as he walked in the temple. After him again with their everlastingly tricky questions. *His authority was still bothering them.* By what authority did he do the things he did? Who gave him this authority? I can imagine Jesus sighed wearily, but his mind was razor sharp: "I am going to ask you a question," he replied, "and if you answer me I will tell you what authority I have for what I do. The baptism of John, now—did it come from Heaven or was it purely human? Tell me that" (Phillips). The learned men argued with each other, figuring a way out: If they said John's baptism came from Heaven, they knew Jesus would say, "Then, why didn't you believe in him?" They knew if they said John's baptism was only humanly devised, their answer would infuriate the people who still believed that John was a true prophet of God. They settled for a noncommital, safe answer: "We don't know."

Of course, Jesus won the skirmish, but their determination to be rid of him once and for all increased. He was not protecting himself in any way at any turn.

CHAPTER 12

vv. 28 through 31

And one of the scribes came, and having heard them reasoning together, and perceiving that he had answered them well, asked him, Which is the first commandment of all? And Jesus answered him, The first of all the commandments is, Hear, O Israel; the Lord our God is one Lord: And thou shalt love the Lord thy God with all thy heart, and with all thy soul, and with all thy mind, and with all thy strength: this is the first commandment. And the second is like, namely this, Thou shalt love thy neighbour as thyself. There is none other commandment greater than these.

This chapter is one long series of trick questions aimed at causing the Lord to "hang himself." As always, he used them creatively—to instruct, to reveal. This is one of the more provocative examples: One clever scribe, figuring that if he could get the Master to favor one Commandment given to Moses over another, he would trap him. Jesus answered by quoting a scripture familiar to them (Deuteronomy 6: 4, 5), which boils all the Commandments down to two which are inclusive. He remained true to what he knew to be fact and still met them on ground where they could feel familiar.

vv. 32, 34

And the scribe said unto him, Well, Master, thou hast said the truth: . . . And no man after that durst ask him any question.

This is a marvelous passage! Marvelous in its succinctness. In its possible hidden meanings. The clever scribe commented upon Jesus' definition of the true Commandments of God this surprising way: "I am well answered . . . You are absolutely right when you say that there is one God and no other God exists but him;

and to love him with the whole of our hearts, the whole of our intelligence and the whole of our energy, and to love our neighbors as ourselves is infinitely more important than all these burnt offerings and sacrifices" (Phillips).

Jesus must have looked deeply into the scribe's heart for a moment, because he said to him: " 'You are not far from the kingdom of God!' After this, no one felt like asking him any more questions" (Phillips). Why didn't they? Jesus had struck a nerve. He had won in the manner of love, not of conquest. What he said had struck the man's inner being. *No one dared risk such exposure after that.*

I can't help wondering how closely this interesting passage has been studied, especially by those who insist upon a confession of sin in a man *before* he can be considered close to the Kingdom of God. Jesus seemed to use the opposite approach. Certainly here. He saw a spark of hope in this man and fanned it. He not only accomplished what had seemed impossible, i.e., to silence his questioners, but he deftly nudged a man toward hope.

CHAPTER 13

v. 11

But when they shall lead you, and deliver you up, take no thought beforehand what ye shall speak, neither do ye premeditate: but whatsoever shall be given you in that hour, that speak ye: for it is not ye that speak, but the Holy Ghost.

Jesus never hesitated to tell them things that were spiritually "over their heads," beyond their current experience. It seems to me he counted heavily on *some* of his words, at least, falling into their subconscious minds, to be brought up and used later. As he warned them of their trials ahead, he told them (as though they had been already taught concerning the work of the Holy Spirit) that they were not to worry about what they would say to the authorities, "for it is not ye that speak, but the Holy Ghost." *Remember, Pentecost had not yet occurred.* Jesus knew it *would* occur, though, and that you and I would be reading his words long after.

CHAPTER 14

vv. 6, 7

And Jesus said, Let her alone; why trouble ye her? she hath wrought a good work on me.

For ye have the poor with you always, and whensoever ye will ye may do them good: but me ye have not always.

Mark, in spite of his brevity, has clarified something here. In his version of the Gospel account, Mark reports that Jesus did not settle for saying merely that the poor we always have with us. Mark adds: ". . . and whensoever ye will, ye may do them good: but me ye have not always."

". . . whensoever ye will ye may do them good: . . ." We are always able to help the poor. Most of us don't think so, but if we believed what Jesus said here, we would not only stop fighting poverty programs, we could begin to make them unnecessary!

v. 8

She hath done what she could: she is come aforehand to anoint my body to the burying.

"She hath done what she could: . . ." One of the Lord's tenderest statements. I try sometimes to imagine how this woman felt when he defended and encouraged her, appreciated her, said she would be memorialized "wheresoever this gospel shall be preached. . . ." Her heart had directed her to do a beautiful and good thing, and God noticed.

vv. 30, 31

And Jesus saith unto him, Verily I say unto thee, That this day, even in this night, before the cock crow twice, thou shalt deny me thrice. But he spake the more vehemently, If I should die with thee, I will not deny thee in any wise. Likewise also said they all.

It is interesting that Mark writes that even after Jesus told Peter he would deny his Master three times before the cock crowed, Peter argued with him. Mark also reports, "Likewise also said they all." Peter, apparently, was not the only disciple who lacked self-knowledge.

v. 40

And when he returned, he found them asleep again, (for their eyes were heavy,) neither wist they what to answer him.

They must have sat up blinking at him, totally unable to think of a word to say for themselves.

vv. 50 through 52

And they all forsook him, and fled. And there followed him a certain young man, having a linen cloth cast about his naked body; and the young men laid hold on him: And he left the linen cloth, and fled from them naked.

It is said that this young man who lost his cloak was John Mark, the author of this Gospel. Tradition says that the disciples and Jesus ate their Passover supper together in the upstairs room of John Mark's mother's house. It all fits together. Even though Mark was a young man, he experienced the shame of that flight for more than one reason! We know from this, though, that he saw the arrest. His telling is firsthand.

v. 54

And Peter followed him afar off, even into the palace of the high priest: and he sat with the servants, and warmed himself at the fire.

Dear, miserable Peter. He fled, too, but not far. At least he followed Jesus at a safe distance. Not commendable, but he did follow; he did stay around.

v. 69

And a maid saw him again, and began to say to them that stood by, This is one of them.

Do you like it said of you that you are "one of them?" How do you react to it? When this was said of Peter, he was "warming himself," protecting himself. Why are we embarrassed to be called "one of them"—Christian?

For the same reason, perhaps, that Peter was ashamed? Because he resembled his Master so little? We need to be perceptive here. We will none of us ever *act like Jesus* on this earth. Shouldn't we accept the joy of being known as "one of them"? And not cringe, directing attention to our inadequacies?

v. 72

> *And the second time the cock crew. And Peter called to mind the word that Jesus said unto him, Before the cock crow twice, thou shalt deny me thrice. And when he thought thereon, he wept.*

Mark throws extra light here: "And when he *thought thereon,* he wept." If only we *thought* more.

CHAPTER 15

vv. 3, 4, 5

> *And the chief priests accused him of many things: but he answered nothing. And Pilate asked him again, saying, Answerest thou nothing? . . . But Jesus yet answered nothing; so that Pilate marvelled.*

Jesus' silence finally caused Pilate to marvel. The strength of God was in it.

v. 15

> *And so Pilate, willing to content the people, . . .*

Pilate, like many of us today, was simply "willing to content the people." We brush over this weakness. It is a serious sin, no matter what our work or calling. It, more than anything else, goes on delivering Jesus into the hands of his enemies.

v. 21

And they compel one Simon a Cyrenian, who passed by, coming out of the country, the father of Alexander and Rufus, to bear his cross.

Wouldn't you like to know if Simon, the Cyrenian, *willingly* helped Jesus bear his cross?

v. 31

. . . He saved others; himself he cannot save.

Himself he *would* not save. We were all too important to him.

v. 39

And when the centurion, which stood over against him, saw that he so cried out, and gave up the ghost, he said, Truly this man was the Son of God.

Do you ever wonder why the centurion began to believe Jesus was the Son of God from having heard his last, loud cry when he "gave up the ghost?" Was it something in that voice? Perhaps a ring of triumph? Triumph mingled with the ending of a creative human life? Even as Jesus died, he drew this man to him. I learn from thinking on this one seldom-mentioned incident in the Great Enactment of love.

vv. 44, 45

And Pilate marvelled if he were already dead: and calling unto him the centurion, he asked him whether he had been any while dead. And when he knew it of the centurion, he gave the body to Joseph.

It is interesting to realize that it was the centurion whom Pilate called to make sure Jesus was dead. The centurion's job, apparently, was to watch the Crucified closely. He became a believer by doing it.

CHAPTER 16
vv. 4, 5

And when they looked, they saw that the stone was rolled away: for it was very great. And entering into the sepulchre, they saw a young man sitting on the right side, clothed in a long white garment; and they were affrighted.

Matthew says the angel rolled away the stone. Mark says it was already rolled away when the women came to care for his body. No matter. The important thing is that the tomb was empty. Jesus did not have to wait for the stone to be rolled away in order to walk out.

vv. 9 through 11

Now when Jesus was risen early the first day of the week, he appeared first to Mary Magdalene, out of whom he had cast seven devils. And she went and told them that had been with him, as they mourned and wept. And they, when they had heard that he was alive, and had been seen of her, believed not.

Did Mary Magdalene run ahead and so meet Jesus, the risen Lord, first? I like to think she did. He had done so much for her. Her need had been so great, her love drove her to hurry back to him "at the rising of the sun." She must have gotten there first and she must have been the first to run, breathless, to tell his disciples. But she was, to the men, merely a talkative woman. They did not believe her.

vv. 12, 13

After that he appeared in another form unto two of them, as they walked, and went into the country. And they went and told it unto the residue: neither believed they them.

The disciples' lack of faith was not altogether due to the fact that Mary of Magdala was a mere woman. The "two of them" to whom Jesus appeared (Luke's Gospel) on the road to Emmaus were men. They told the other disciples and were also doubted.

vv. 14, 15

Afterward he appeared unto the eleven as they sat at meat, and upbraided them with their unbelief and hardness of heart, because they believed not them which had seen him after he was risen. And he said unto them, Go ye into all the world, and preach the gospel to every creature.

As he had always done, Jesus did what he had to do. He went straight to the disciples, (locked up safely in a room, eating) and upbraided them for their little faith. But *he went,* longing for them to be comforted, to know. And the fact that they had been hard to convince did not stop him from giving them his great commission: "Go ye into all the world and preach the gospel to every creature." He has never waited for us to "advance" to a particular spiritual state before sending us out. This false idea is behind our silly disillusionment when a "Christian leader" falls on his or her face. God does not send "supreme beings"; he sends faulty men and women—like the eleven who deserted him in his hour of greatest need. If he waited for our "perfection," there would be no one to go!

Saint Luke

And they were both righteous before God, walking in all the commandments and ordinances of the Lord blameless.

It must be realized that both Zacharias and his wife, Elisabeth, were righteous people before God; considered by God to be "blameless." This is important to the impact of the next considered verses.

vv. 8, 11, 13 through 17

And it came to pass, that while he executed the priest's office before God in the order of his course, . . . there appeared unto him an angel of the Lord . . . the angel said unto him. Fear not, Zacharias: for thy prayer is heard; and thy wife Elisabeth shall bear thee a son, and thou shalt call his name John. And thou shalt have joy and gladness; and many shall rejoice at his birth. For he shall be great in the sight of the Lord, and shall drink neither wine nor strong drink; and he shall be filled with the Holy Ghost, even from his mother's womb. And many of the children of Israel shall he turn to the Lord their God. And he shall go before him in the spirit and power of Elias, to turn the hearts of the fathers to the children, and the disobedient to the wisdom of the just; to make ready a people prepared for the Lord.

When the angel of the Lord came to Zacharias, he spared no effort to make himself understood. He even encouraged the old priest by reminding him that he and his elderly wife would "have joy and gladness." He explained the mission of the son to be born to them in their declining years. Nothing was omitted. God knew it would come as a shock to them both, since they were too old to have a child. And so he went the whole way to explain.

v. 18

And Zacharias said unto the angel, Whereby shall I know this? for I am an old man, and my wife well stricken in years.

In spite of God's care to make himself clear, in spite of the fact that Zacharias was considered "blameless" before God, the old man's first question was riddled with doubt. He did not ask "How can this happen?" as Mary asked when told by the angel that she would bear a son by the Holy Spirit. Zacharias had not accepted what the angel said as fact at all. He asked: "Whereby shall I know this?" Not "How can this be?" But, "How am I to know what you say is true?"

vv. 19, 20

And the angel answering said unto him, I am Gabriel, that stand in the presence of God; and am sent to speak unto thee, and to shew thee these glad tidings. And, behold, thou shalt be dumb, and not able to speak, until the day that these things shall be performed, because thou believest not my words, which shall be fulfilled in their season.

The angel Gabriel identified himself as one who stood in the presence of God, and immediately informed the doubting Zacharias that he would be unable to speak one more word until the day his son would be born. There are those who believe God struck the old priest dumb as punishment for his doubt. Others theorize that such deep and sudden doubt can silence a man's tongue. Still others (and I tend toward this) feel the shock was too much for the old man's emotional make-up. He had a psychosomatic reaction to the stunning news. I lean toward this theory simply because I do not believe God punishes in such ways. I believe he punishes by love and that is, in the long run, more severe and brings more lasting results. On the other hand, I can accept the fact that God gave Zacharias a temporary respite from speech—not so much as a punishment—but so that he would not be able to discourage his equally ancient wife, Elisabeth. After all, she had the difficult time ahead, and doubt caught from her husband could make it still more difficult. Elisabeth needed desperately to be free from doubt, to be able to receive the rest and strength that come from complete trust in God. Perhaps God was merely guaranteeing her peace of mind by keeping Zacharias' mouth shut. The fact of his inability to speak could also be the convincing factor for Elisabeth that he had truly seen and talked with the angel of the Lord. As with so many other provocative passages in the Bible, it is a waste to permit oneself to be sidetracked into controversy. Too much of life-changing importance is about to happen!

vv. 26 through 34

And in the sixth month the angel Gabriel was sent from God unto a city of Galilee, named Nazareth, To a virgin espoused to a man whose name was Joseph, of the house of David; and the virgin's name was Mary. And the angel came in unto her, and said, Hail, thou that art highly favoured, the Lord is with thee: blessed art thou among women. And when she saw him, she was troubled at his saying, and cast in her mind what manner of salutation this should be. And the angel said unto her, Fear not, Mary: for thou hast found favour with God. And, behold, thou shalt conceive in thy womb, and bring forth a son, and shalt call his name Jesus. He shall be great, and shall be called the Son of the Highest: and the Lord God shall give unto him the throne of his father David: And he shall reign over the house of Jacob for ever; and of his kingdom there shall be no end. Then said Mary unto the angel, How shall this be, seeing I know not a man?

Six months later, when Elisabeth was well along in her pregnancy, the same angel, Gabriel, appeared to her young cousin, Mary, in the hill town of Nazareth with news so startling that a much older and wiser woman might understandably have fainted or flown into hysterics. Not Mary. Of course, she was perturbed, unable to imagine what such a lofty message could mean. After all, she was only an insignificant young girl, about to be married to Joseph, the kindly carpenter. How could *she* be singled out to be addressed as "blessed . . . among women"? What Gabriel was really saying was that the Messiah was coming and that he would be *her* child. Now, Jewish women for years had been praying and hoping for this signal honor. I doubt that Mary had done this. In her estimation, she would be the last person God would choose. Yet, here was the angel telling her that even before she had known a man, she would conceive a child who would be called "the Son of the Highest"! But, in all her shock and confusion, Mary remembered the angel had said, "The Lord is with thee." For Mary, whose simple faith had never wavered, *this was enough.* So, her first question was full of trust: "How shall this be, seeing I know not a man?" She did not ask, as Zacharias had asked, how she could know this was the truth. *She asked for no proof.* Just how was it going to happen? A logical question. In effect: "I believe you, but please tell me how this will take place."

vv. 35 through 38

And the angel answered and said unto her, The Holy Ghost shall come upon thee, and the power of the Highest shall overshadow thee: therefore also that holy thing which shall be born of thee shall be called the Son of God. And, behold, thy cousin Elisabeth, she hath also conceived a son in her old age: and this is the sixth month with her, who was called barren. For with God nothing shall be impossible. And Mary said, Behold the handmaid of the Lord; be it unto me according to thy word. And the angel departed from her.

And the angel told her carefully, clearly. He also explained about her elderly cousin, Elisabeth; that she was in her sixth month with child. He did not go into the purpose of John's birth. God knew this would be

too much for the young, awe-struck girl to take in.
Rather, Gabriel told her about Elisabeth more to assure
her that ". . . with God nothing shall be impossible."
For Mary this was enough. Her answer to Gabriel holds
the key to releasing God's power for us all: "Behold the
handmaid of the Lord: be it unto me according to thy
word." Phillips translates her words this way: "I belong
to the Lord, body and soul . . . let it happen as you say."

vv. 39, 40 (Read through v. 45.)

*And Mary arose in those days, and went into the hill
country with haste, into a city of Juda; And entered into
the house of Zacharias, and saluted Elisabeth.*

Mary, needing someone to share her awe and her joy,
hurried, as soon as possible, to Elisabeth's home. Elisabeth would understand. Her old cousin, too, was shut
away from the unknowing world by the miracle of God
taking place in her. No one but Elisabeth could possibly
know how she felt. And when Mary reached her cousin's
house, even before she had a chance to tell what had
happened, Elisabeth's baby leaped for joy within her
and God verified his plan to them in a moment of intense joy and praise. Before his birth, Elisabeth called
Jesus her Lord!

These two women needed each other and God saw to
it that they could share the wonder together. He is
always aware that there are times when his glory is too
much for us. This, of course, is why he permits only
occasional glimpses of it. We could not bear the wonder
otherwise.

vv. 62 through 64

And they made signs to his father, how he would have him called. And he asked for a writing table, and wrote, saying, His name is John. And they marvelled all. And his mouth was opened immediately, and his tongue loosed, and he spake, and praised God.

As soon as Zacharias had agreed with Elisabeth that the angel of the Lord had named the baby John, instead of Zacharias, the old priest could speak again. And he really spoke! In words inspired by God himself, he prophesied the future life of his son and his role in announcing the coming of the "dayspring from on high"—Mary's child, not yet born.

Chapter 2

vv. 1 through 7

And it came to pass in those days, that there went out a decree from Caesar Augustus, that all the world should be taxed. (And this taxing was first made when Cyrenius was governor of Syria.) And all went to be taxed, every one into his own city. And Joseph also went up from Galilee, out of the city of Nazareth, into Judaea, unto the city of David, which is called Bethlehem; (because he was of the house and lineage of David:) To be taxed with Mary his espoused wife, being great with child. And so it was, that, while they were there, the days were accomplished that she should be delivered. And she brought forth her first-born son, and wrapped him in swaddling clothes, and laid him in a manger; because there was no room for them in the inn.

Matthew has explained the turmoil in gentle Joseph's heart when he learned that Mary was "great with child"

before he had known her. Joseph took the way of love
and boldly went to his native city of Bethlehem with
his expectant wife, to be taxed. The gossip back in
Nazareth must have made the air crackle! But God had
spoken to them both, had acted within them both, and
they went on without fear. Not only did Joseph show
his strong faith in God, his quality of character; he
showed only the greatest tenderness toward Mary. She
was going to be as comfortable as a woman could be in
a stable, when her son was born. I am sure Joseph left
nothing undone that could be done for her. And God,
as always, was making creative use of even the crude,
makeshift surroundings. It was a chilly night; the houses
and inns were poorly heated. But Mary had the warmth
of the bodies of the animals near her in the stable. God
wastes nothing. Not even our hardships.

vv. 8 through 18

*And there were in the same country shepherds abiding
in the field, keeping watch over their flock by night.
And, lo, the angel of the Lord came upon them, and the
glory of the Lord shone round about them: and they
were sore afraid. And the angel said unto them, Fear
not: for, behold, I bring you good tidings of great joy,
which shall be to all people. For unto you is born this
day in the city of David a Saviour, which is Christ the
Lord. And this shall be a sign unto you; Ye shall find
the babe wrapped in swaddling clothes, lying in a
manger. And suddenly there was with the angel a multitude of the heavenly host praising God, and saying,
Glory to God in the highest, and on earth peace, good
will toward men.*

And it came to pass, as the angels were gone away from them into heaven, the shepherds said to one another, Let us now go even unto Bethlehem, and see this thing which is come to pass, which the Lord hath made known unto us. And they came with haste, and found Mary, and Joseph, and the babe lying in a manger. And when they had seen it, they made known abroad the saying which was told them concerning this child. And all they that heard it wondered at those things which were told them by the shepherds.

God did not come into the world as a Man, with enormous advance publicity and noisy fanfare. But neither did he make his entrance among us with no signs of confirmation. It would have done little good if he had announced his arrival elaborately to the world. The world did not understand him, would not have grasped his meaning. And so, God spread the word that the Saviour was here, that redemption was at hand, by the same means he still uses: through the few people who live close enough to him to understand something of his purposes. God made his announcements to those who believed in him. First, Zacharias and Elisabeth, who spread the word concerning the mission God had planned for their son, John. Then, Mary and Joseph. Now, in these verses, he is telling the simple shepherds on the hillside outside Bethlehem. They were all believers, who took him at his word. The "remnant" as Bible scholars say. And to the shepherds, God made his joyful announcement in a heavenly choral concert! Were these plain, working men the only ones who were able to hear the celestial chorus that night? I wonder.

At any rate, once they heard and saw, the shepherds "made known abroad the saying which was told them concerning this child." God did not come unannounced. He simply made his announcement only to those who could and would hear.

v. 19

> *But Mary kept all these things, and pondered them in her heart.*

Mary apparently talked little about what had happened. She didn't need to. God did not choose her to spread the glad news, he chose her to bear his Son. I try at times, but I can't imagine what she "pondered in her heart." Oh, we can know some of it, I suppose. "Mother things" certainly. This was God's Son, but it was her son, too. At any rate, Mary had too much to think about to talk.

v. 30 (Read vv. 22 through 33.)

> *For mine eyes have seen thy salvation, . . .*

God evidently was making his announcement directly to the hearts and minds of other devout Jews, too. I have always loved this passage concerning old Simeon, waiting to die, but knowing he would not die until he had seen the Lord's Christ. Mary and Joseph were not famous people. I doubt that anyone but God knew they were in the temple that day, but he knew, and he sent old Simeon there *to see Jesus.* The most meaningful part of this incident to me is what Simeon said when he took the Baby in his arms: "Lord, now lettest thou thy servant depart in peace, according to thy word; *for mine eyes have seen thy salvation."* He could have said: ". . . for mine eyes have seen the Christ." *The words are interchangeable,* but how seldom we think of them that way! We have compartmentalized, as is our dear, foolish delight. Most of us think of our "salvation" as a *thing,* a *process,* a *happening.* Jesus Christ himself *is* our salvation! When one sees him, one sees salvation. Surely, this thoughless compartmentalizing is the reason so many sincere, fearful Christians speak of "losing their salvation." Can one "lose" God? Didn't he say he would be with us always? That he would never leave us or forsake us? "Salvation" cannot die because God cannot die. Old Simeon had it straight, and Mary and Joseph marveled. I don't blame them.

v. 49 (Read vv. 42 through 52.)

And he said unto them, How is it that ye sought me? wist ye not that I must be about my Father's business?

Luke wrote this episode of Jesus' conversing with the learned men in the temple with great skill. Mary must have told him about it. I can almost hear her: "He had always been such a good boy, so considerate. In all his twelve years, I hadn't had a moment's worry over him until that day. Joseph and I were frantic! We searched everywhere. Because Jesus had always been such an obedient and thoughtful little boy, we were sure something dreadful had happened to him. And then we found him, sitting right there in the midst of those learned doctors, both answering their profound questions and asking his own of them! As calm and mature as you please. And they were treating him as though he were a respected adult. Dr. Luke, they were *all* astonished at his learning! I was proud of him, of course, but I couldn't help scolding him a little. We had been so frightened. And when I asked him why he had worried us so, he answered in the strangest words. Oh, he wasn't sharp with me. His voice was quiet and gentle, as though he were praying that I would somehow understand: 'How is it that ye sought me? Wist ye not that I must be about my Father's business?' Well, I can tell you, neither Joseph nor I understood at all, but after that, we all went home together and never again was he anything but what he had been before—a good, thoughtful, obedient boy." You can be sure Mary never forgot the incident, but evidently she said no more about it then. She just kept all his "sayings in her heart." Jesus grew up in a typical hill-country town, in healthy surroundings, close to nature—away from the dirt and bustle of Jerusalem or Bethlehem. How like God to arrange this. He wanted him to be reared in naturalness, sensitive to the sky and the sea and the olive trees and the grapevines and the wheat fields. He worked in his earthly father's carpentry shop with his hands. It was hard, manual work, but creative. Surely, God chose the right earthly father for him. Joseph was a kind man, strong, full of faith, and gentle. And the Boy Jesus was the Son of God. It is no wonder he "increased in wisdom and stature, and in favour with God and man."

CHAPTER 3

vv. 1 through 6 (Read through v. 18.)

Now in the fifteenth year of the reign of Tiberius Caesar, Pontius Pilate being governor of Judaea, and Herod being tetrarch of Galilee, and his brother Philip tetrarch of Ituraea and of the region of Trachonitis, and Lysanias the tetrarch of Abilene, Annas and Caiphas being the high priests, the word of God came unto John the son of Zacharias in the wilderness. And he came into all the country about Jordan, preaching the baptism of repentance for the remission of sins; As it is written in the book of the words of Esaias the prophet, saying, The voice of one crying in the wilderness, Prepare ye the way of the Lord, make his paths straight. Every valley shall be filled, and every mountain and hill shall be brought low; and the crooked shall be made straight, and the rough ways shall be made smooth; And all flesh shall see the salvation of God. . . .

Luke has set his scene well again. We know who is in political power; we know the date and something of the times. At the end of Chapter 1, Luke had written of John: "And the child grew, and waxed strong in spirit, and was in the deserts till the day of his shewing unto Israel." John, born of aged parents, had grown up in very unnatural conditions compared with the childhood of Jesus. He was, according to Mark, "clothed with camel's hair, and with a girdle of a skin about his loins; and he did eat locusts and wild honey. . . ." John was a totally dedicated man with a mission straight from God. No man on earth had been given such responsibility, and John fulfilled his calling. But he was considered an eccentric, an aesthete, and compared with Jesus, he was. This is in no way a deprecation of John. Unless a man is the only begotten Son of God, as Jesus was, such a mission would so occupy him that he would have no energy left for the normal pursuits of life! John the Baptist has intrigued me as a human being for years. I admire him, I pity him, I'm sure I would have found him uncomfortable socially. His life was so taken up with his mission (most of which was new to him) that there was no time to learn social niceties, to enter into comfortable human relationships. As it appeared to him, he had no choice but to deny himself all these things and live alone in the desert, trying every minute to learn more of what was expected of him.

So here is John, as a grown man, in Luke's graphic account, mingling with throngs of people, away from his beloved desert and his privacy, embarked on his mission at last, still pouring himself out for God. And doing so with power and insight and enormous vigor. Stretching himself, as it were, across the wide gap between the semidarkness of the Old Testament toward the bright light of the New. Utterly convinced of the power of the living God. Shouting to the crowds that thronged around him that "God is able of these stones to raise up children unto Abraham!" Using foreshadowings of the kind of practical, Christian teaching that concerns human behavior, relationships. (See verses 11, 12, 13, 14.) Proclaiming that "one mightier than I cometh, the latchet of whose shoes I am unworthy to unloose." As God planned it, Elisabeth's son was announcing the coming of Mary's Son, who would make the crooked straight and the rough ways smooth.

vv. 19, 20

But Herod the tetrarch, being reproved by him for Herodias his brother Philip's wife, and for all the evils which Herod had done, Added yet this above all, that he shut up John in prison.

Just before Jesus appeared to take his place in line to be baptized by John, Herod (because of John's condemnation for the King's love affair with his brother's wife) was being pressured by his mistress to shut John up in prison. The Baptist baptized Jesus, the Holy Spirit led Jesus into the wilderness to be tempted and tried, and John was silenced—shut away from the sky and the wind and the sun he loved so much—by four close, thick, damp stone walls, never to be free again in this world.

CHAPTER 4

vv. 14, 15

And Jesus returned in the power of the Spirit into Galilee: and there went out a fame of him through all the region round about. And he taught in their synagogues, being glorified of all.

After his baptism by John in the Jordan, after John's imprisonment by Herod, after his own temptation-filled forty days in the wilderness alone, Jesus "returned in the power of the Spirit into Galilee." His earthly

ministry had begun, and it is interesting to observe that
in these early days, he was "glorified by all." His tormentors had not yet started their pursuit of him.

vv. 16 through 21, 28 through 30

*And he came to Nazareth, where he had been brought
up: and, as his cutom was, he went into the synagogue
on the sabbath day, and stood up for to read. And there
was delivered unto him the book of the prophet Esaias.
And when he had opened the book, he found the place
where it was written, The Spirit of the Lord is upon
me, because he hath anointed me to preach the gospel to
the poor; he hath sent me to heal the broken-hearted,
to preach deliverance to the captives, and recovering of
sight to the blind, to set at liberty them that are bruised,
To preach the acceptable year of the Lord. And he
closed the book, and he gave it again to the minister, and
sat down. And the eyes of all them that were in the
synagogue were fastened on him. And he began to say
unto them, This day is this scripture fulfilled in your
ears. . . . And all they in the synagogue, when they heard
these things, were filled with wrath, And rose up, and
thrust him out of the city, and led him unto the brow
of the hill whereon their city was built, that they might
cast him down headlong. But he passing through the
midst of them went his way.*

Apparently his troubles did not begin until he went
back to his home town of Nazareth. Even here, for the
first moments of his teaching in the familiar old synagogue—his audience made up of his friends and neighbors and relatives—things went rather well. But as he
bore in upon their precious traditions, as he began to
shake their *status quo*, they turned on him and at-

tempted to push him headlong over a cliff! "But he passing through the midst of them went his way."

CHAPTER 5

v. 4 (Read through v. 11.)

Now when he had left speaking, he said unto Simon, Launch out into the deep, and let down your nets for a draught.

This is a story none of the other Gospel accounts tells. Its impact to me is in the fact that Jesus uses whatever is at hand, whatever is familiar, most understandable, to draw his disciples to him. Peter and Andrew and James and John "understood" about fishing.

vv. 36 through 39

And he spake also a parable unto them; No man putteth a piece of a new garment upon an old; if otherwise, then both the new maketh a rent, and the piece that was taken out of the new agreeth not with the old. And no man putteth new wine into old bottles; else the new wine will burst the bottles, and be spilled, and the bottles shall perish. But new wine must be put into new bottles; and both are preserved. No man also having drunk old wine straightway desireth new: for he saith, The old is better.

Jesus had grown up simply, knowing about grapes and harvest and the making of wine and the use of leather wine bottles. He did not grow up in luxury. Putting patches on worn garments was no new thing to him.

CHAPTER 6

v. 12

And it came to pass in those days, that he went out into a mountain to pray, and continued all night in prayer to God.

The burden of his days was so heavy, even Jesus could not have managed without longer and more frequent times of prayer with the Father than most of us ever experience.

vv. 41, 42

And why beholdest thou the mote that is in thy brother's eye, but perceivest not the beam that is in thine own eye? Either how canst thou say to thy brother, Brother, let me pull out the mote that is in thine eye, when thou thyself beholdest not the beam that is in thine own eye? Thou hypocrite, cast out first the beam out of thine own eye, and then shalt thou see clearly to pull out the mote that is in thy brother's eye.

His humor is keen here, but beneath it—truth. Isn't it really ridiculous for a gossip to condemn a man for drinking too much?

CHAPTER 7

v. 9 (Read vv. 1 through 10.)

When Jesus heard these things, he marvelled at him, and turned him about, and said unto the people that followed him, I say unto you, I have not found so great faith, no, not in Israel.

This is a strong story. And with a surprise twist at the end. Not the healing of the beloved servant. When Jesus healed, it was no surpirse. The surprise is that

Jesus, for once, had a chance to marvel at something! Here was a man—a pagan centurion—who understood authority and obedience. The centurion's marvelous simplicity here merits much attention.

CHAPTER 8
vv. 1, 2, 3

And it came to pass afterward, that he went throughout every city and village, preaching and shewing the glad tidings of the kingdom of God: and the twelve were with him, And certain women, which had been healed of evil spirits and infirmities, Mary called Magdalene, out of whom went seven devils, And Joanna the wife of Chuza Herod's steward, and Susanna, and many others, which ministered unto him of their substance.

Most of us think only of Mary of Magdala when we think of the woman from whom Jesus "cast seven devils." Mary would, I'm sure, be the first to admit that it was she. But evidently he was followed and ministered to (from their own resources) by other women, some of whose needs had been as great and as shocking as the Magdalene's. One of these was Joanna, the wife of Herod's steward. Another was an otherwise anonymous woman named Susanna—all of whom were anything but anonymous to Jesus.

v. 9

And his disciples asked him, saying, What might this parable be?

Whatever the full meaning of the parable of the sower might be (and here Jesus gave his men an interpretation), it is evident that he knew as he worked (and accepted the fact) that all the seed he dropped would *not* fall on good ground. We can learn from this acceptance. Jesus was never anxious, he never pressured anyone into the Kingdom. His is a much wider view than ours can be, but perhaps we should accept his seeming relaxation in the midst of his labors by faith, and make it our own.

CHAPTER 9
vv. 1, 2

Then he called his twelve disciples together, and gave them power and authority over all devils, and to cure diseases. And he sent them to preach the kingdom of God, and to heal the sick.

I never cease marveling at the chances God takes. These twelve men seem to have caught on so slowly; their faith appears so weak, their love so limited. And yet he sent them out in his name to cast out devils and cure diseases! As he sends us. We tremble in fear for the reputation of God. Certainly, his view is infinitely broader than ours, infinitely more liberal, because God goes right on taking these bad risks.

v. 9

And Herod said, John have I beheaded: but who is this, of whom I hear such things? And he desired to see him.

Eventually Herod got his chance "to see him," but under very different circumstances (Luke 23: 8, 9).

vv. 10, 11

And the apostles, when they were returned, told him all that they had done. And he took them, and went aside privately into a desert place belonging to the city called Bethsaida. And the people, when they knew it, followed him: and he received them, and spake unto them of the kingdom of God, and healed them that had need of healing.

When the disciples returned from their first trip without the Master, of course, they were full of stories of the wonders that had happened because of the authority he had given them. Jesus attempted to take them away where they could be alone and rest and pray—to give them a much needed recharging for what he knew lay ahead. But, as usual, the crowds came with their needs and were met, as usual, with his compassion, his attention, his healing. *And* the miracle of the multiplied food for their hunger.

v. 18

And it came to pass, as he was alone praying, his disciples were with him: and he asked them, saying, Whom say the people that I am?

At last he is alone with his disciples at prayer. And Luke tells us it is in the midst of prayer that he asks the one vital question: "Whom do men say that I am?" Perhaps Peter's answer could be, in part, correct because of the wonders he had just experienced through the authority given him by this Man who could not be like any other man on earth. Who *had* to be "The Christ of God."

v. 36

And when the voice was past, Jesus was found alone.
And they kept it close, and told no man in those days
any of those things which they had seen.

The three who went with Jesus to the Mount of
Transfiguration were growing. It must have been very
difficult for them to "keep it close," to tell no man what
they had seen there. It would have been easy to boast.
After all, they were the three he chose to witness it. We
have no record that they did anything but keep still
about it.

v. 51

And it came to pass, when the time was come that he
should be received up, he stedfastly set his face to go to
Jerusalem,

Another "transfiguration" must have appeared in his
face. The quality of flint showed. His whole will was
"stedfastly set" to walk directly into his agony, even to
the Cross. If one has not seen the stern side of the face
of Jesus Christ, one has not yet seen him.

vv. 52 through 56

And sent messengers before his face: and they went,
and entered into a village of the Samaritans, to make
ready for him. And they did not receive him, because
his face was as though he would go to Jerusalem. And
when his disciples James and John saw this, they said,
Lord, wilt thou that we command fire to come down
from heaven, and consume them, even as Elias did? But
he turned, and rebuked them, and said, Ye know not
what manner of spirit ye are of. For the Son of man is

not come to destroy men's lives, but to save them. And they went to another village.

When they came to the Samaritan village en route to Jerusalem, they were turned out. No one would receive them. The seven-hundred-year-old antagonism between the Samaritans and the orthodox Jews still held. The Jews despised the Samaritans as aliens who claimed the privileges of Israel. The despising worked both ways. Just knowing Jesus was on his way to Jerusalem (the city they hated) was enough to cause the Samaritans to refuse him shelter. James and John, whom Jesus had rightly surnamed Sons of Thunder, thundered! They were so angry they wanted to burn up the village, using Elijah (II Kings 1:10) as their authority. Jesus rebuked them. They were now living under *his* authority! And "the Son of Man is not come to destroy men's lives, but to save them." Weary as they were, they plodded on to another village for the night. We had better not use even Scripture to back up our anger, if it seems unlike Jesus.

vv. 57, 58

And it came to pass, that, as they went in the way, a certain man said unto him, Lord, I will follow thee withersoever thou goest. And Jesus said unto him, Foxes have holes, and birds of the air have nests; but the Son of man hath not where to lay his head.

This man obviously was not a disciple, but wanted to be. Jesus wanted him to count the cost first. He would have to be willing, as the Master was, to enjoy fewer privileges than foxes enjoy.

vv. 59 through 62

And he said unto another, Follow me. But he said, Lord, suffer me first to go and bury my father. Jesus said unto him, Let the dead bury their dead: but go thou and preach the kingdom of God. And another also said, Lord, I will follow thee; but let me first go bid them farewell, which are at home at my house. And Jesus said unto him, No man, having put his hand to the plow, and looking back, is fit for the kingdom of God.

These are hard sayings. And yet, we must never lose sight of the fact that only Jesus knew these men as they really were. Perhaps if the one had gone off to bury his father, he would never have come back. The same may have been true of the man who wanted to go home for a tearful farewell to his family. The family pull may have been stronger than the pull toward Christ. Jesus knew in detail. He *still* knows in detail.

CHAPTER 10

vv. 1 through 3

After these things the Lord appointed other seventy also, and sent them two and two before his face into every city and place, whither he himself would come. Therefore said he unto them, The harvest truly is great, but the labourers are few: pray ye therefore the Lord of the harvest, that he would send forth labourers into his harvest. Go your ways: behold, I send you forth as lambs among wolves.

The time was growing short. His missionary enterprise had to be enlarged. Seventy disciples went out this time—as before, *two by two*. Jesus, even in the face of the enormity of his still unfinished task, bothered to think of the men's need of companionship. Especially since they were being sent "as lambs among wolves."

v. 25 (Read through v. 37.)

And, behold, a certain lawyer stood up, and tempted him, saying, Master, what shall I do to inherit eternal life?

Luke enlarges this episode most helpfully. It is almost as though his lawyer is a different man from Mark's. This is, of course, because two writers see him in differing aspects. All of which can be enlightening rather than confusing to us. Luke includes the parable of the Good Samaritan to enlarge our view and stretch our understanding of loving one's neighbor. Jesus induces the scribe to answer his own question: Who is my neighbor? We see that our neighbor is anyone who needs us. The Good Samaritan story gives the provocative feeling that Jesus was looking ahead to our world of troubled race relations. Remember, the Jews hated the Samaritans and the Samaritans hated the Jews.

CHAPTER 11

v. 33

No man, when he hath lighted a candle, putteth it in a secret place, neither under a bushel, but on a candle-stick, that they which come in may see the light.

It is good to think on the Lord's plain common sense.

v. 34

The light of the body is the eye: therefore when thine eye is single, thy whole body also is full of light; but when thine eye is evil, thy body also is full of darkness.

If we have eyes only for God, we do not miss the needs of the world he loves. "The light of the body is the eye." *We become what we look at.* What gets our attention, gets us. And this includes a steady diet of TV and gossip. If Christ has our attention, we are full of light. His light.

v. 35

Take heed therefore that the light which is in thee be not darkness.

Does this make you think of the tight-mouthed, doctrine-clutching Christians who put their own religious concepts before love? Their doctrine may be perfectly "correct"; to the best of their knowledge, their faith is in Jesus Christ. But he warned, "Take heed therefore that the light which is in thee be not [as] darkness."

The same is true, of course, of the sort of liberal who bends every effort to "show love" to the needy, but who ignores the necessity for redemption in every human heart. The same warning applies: "Take heed therefore that the light which is in thee be not [as] darkness."

CHAPTER 12
vv. 8, 9

Also I say unto you, Whosoever shall confess me be-fore men, him shall the Son of man also confess before the angels of God: But he that denieth me before men shall be denied before the angels of God.

Jesus is not bargaining here. Not making deals. He is

speaking realistically, as always. If we do not confess him as being ours, he cannot confess us as being his. He would be lying if he did.

vv. 27, 28

Consider the lilies how they grow: they toil not, they spin not; and yet I say unto you, that Solomon in all his glory was not arrayed like one of these. If then God so clothe the grass, which is to day in the field, and to morrow is cast into the oven; how much more will he clothe you, O ye of little faith?

I have heard people complain, "Yes, but I'm not a lily. I can't be expected to stand rooted in one spot!" This is not the point. Our western minds are so literal. The lily and the grass merely meet the conditions of growth and they grow. Is this asking too much of us as human beings?

v. 32

Fear not, little flock; for it is your Father's good pleasure to give you the kingdom.

One of the dearest verses in the New Testament. In the whole Bible for that matter. It is seldom used as a verse of comfort. But, how comforting it is! It relaxes me to be thought of by God as one of his "little flock." And to think it is our Father's "good pleasure to give us the kingdom!" Surely, only the unduly troubled mind, the anxious heart, the misinformed, the darkened insight could insult such a Father by *pleading* for what Jesus says gives him "good pleasure."

CHAPTER 13

vv. 10 through 17

And he was teaching in one of the synagogues on the sabbath. And, behold, there was a woman which had a spirit of infirmity eighteen years, and was bowed together, and could in no wise lift up herself. And when Jesus saw her, he called her to him, and said unto her, Woman, thou art loosed from thine infirmity. And he laid his hands on her: and immediately she was made straight, and glorified God. And the ruler of the synagogue answered with indignation, because that Jesus had healed on the sabbath day, and said unto the people, There are six days in which men ought to work: in them therefore come and be healed, and not on the sabbath day. The Lord then answered him, and said, Thou hypocrite, doth not each one of you on the sabbath loose his ox or his ass from the stall, and lead him away to watering? And ought not this woman, being a daughter of Abraham, whom Satan hath bound, lo, these eighteen years, be loosed from this bond on the sabbath day? And when he had said these things, all his adversaries were ashamed: and all the people rejoiced for all the glorious things that were done by him.

Jesus himself called the woman with the bent back from the audience in the synagogue this particular Sabbath day. She did not come to him, *he called her* and healed her. And yet, the infuriated ruler of the synagogue dared not berate Jesus because the audience was so "with" him. Luke gives us a contrast here to the usual heckling of the Master himself. This time the ruler shouted at the *people.*

vv. 18 through 22

Then said he, Unto what is the kingdom of God like? and whereunto shall I resemble it? It is like a grain of mustard seed, which a man took, and cast into his garden; and it grew, and waxed a great tree; and the fowls of the air lodged in the branches of it. And again he said, Whereunto shall I liken the kingdom of God? It is like leaven, which a woman took and hid in three measures of meal, till the whole was leavened. And he went through the cities and villages, teaching, and journeying toward Jerusalem.

The Lord's feeling ran so deep after the incident with the crippled woman he had healed, he seemed to be trying harder and harder to make people understand that the kingdom he preached was not an outer thing governed by laws, but an inner, living organism capable of growth. "What is the kingdom of God like? What illustration can I use to make it plain to you?" And then he likened it to a mustard seed. And again, "What can I say the kingdom of God is like?" And then he likened it to the yeast a woman uses in making bread. We can feel his inner tension grow as he nears Jerusalem. Not for fear of what lay ahead, but for sorrow that the time was growing so short. He is expending his energies almost constantly these days, trying, *trying* to get through to his listeners.

CHAPTER 14

vv. 11 through 14

For whosoever exalteth himself shall be abased; and he that humbleth himself shall be exalted. Then said he also to him that bade him, When thou makest a dinner or a supper, call not thy friends, nor thy brethren, neither thy kinsmen, nor thy rich neighbours; lest they also bid thee again, and a recompence be made thee. But when thou makest a feast, call the poor, the maimed, the lame, the blind: And thou shalt be blessed; for they cannot recompense thee: for thou shalt be recompensed at the resurrection of the just.

Always the glorious paradox of the Gospel. Christ looks through the opposite end of the telescope and sees things and people as they are.

vv. 26, 27

If any man come to me, and hate not his father, and mother, and wife, and children, and brethren, and sisters, yea, and his own life also, he cannot be my disciple. And whosoever doth not bear his cross, and come after me, cannot be my disciple.

Jesus was not about the business of breaking up families. He was about the business of calling men to God, but always, always, he urged them to count the cost of discipleship. These words sound hard. Viewed from *his* vantage point—where the obstacles are *already gone*—they are only freeing.

CHAPTER 15

Note: In this entire chapter, in my opinion, Jesus is attempting, *as the high point of his teaching ministry,* to explain to the people something of the true nature, the seeking, loving heart of his Father. Jesus seems determined to unlock them from their old concept of a vengeful God. The Father *he* comes revealing is one capable of rejoicing when one lost person comes home.

vv. 1 through 7

> *Then drew near unto him all the publicans and sin-ners for to hear him. And the Pharisees and scribes murmured, saying, This man receiveth sinners, and eateth with them. And he spake this parable unto them, saying, What man of you, having an hundred sheep, if he lose one of them, doth not leave the ninety and nine in the wilderness, and go after that which is lost, until he find it? And when he hath found it, he layeth it on his shoulders, rejoicing. And when he cometh home, he calleth together his friends and neighbours, saying unto them, Rejoice with me; for I have found my sheep which was lost. I say unto you, that likewise joy shall be in heaven over one sinner that repenteth, more than over ninety and nine just persons, which need no repentance.*

Oddly, but not oddly, at the moment of my own turn-ing to Jesus Christ, the old song "The Ninety and Nine" came hauntingly to my mind. I had not heard it in more than twenty-five years. Not since I was a small child and had been popped up on a platform and per-mitted to sing all the verses. But there it was and there God was and there was I, convinced at last, that his heart had been longing over this one lost sheep. His is that kind of heart. God is not partial to sinners who need repentance over those righteous persons who do not. He is simply *concerned over human need.* And when need is met, he rejoices.

vv. 8 through 10

Either what woman having ten pieces of silver, if she lose one piece, doth not light a candle, and sweep the house, and seek diligently till she find it? And when she hath found it, she calleth her friends and her neighbours together, saying, Rejoice with me; for I have found the piece which I had lost. Likewise, I say unto you, there is joy in the presence of the angels of God over one sinner that repenteth.

Here again, the parable of the woman who lost one coin points to the fact of the searching heart of God. For one lost child, the Father will pour out his light, will sweep away obstacles, will diligently seek until that lost child is found. And, because of *what he is like,* he rejoices. The woman's distress over the lost coin does not mean that she did not value the ones she still had.

vv. 25 through 32

Now his elder son was in the field: and as he came and drew nigh to the house, he heard musick and dancing. And he called one of the servants and asked what these things meant. And he said unto him, Thy brother is come; and thy father hath killed the fatted calf, because he hath received him safe and sound. And he was angry, and would not go in: therefore came his father out, and intreated him. And he answering said to his father, Lo, these many years do I serve thee, neither transgressed I at any time thy commandment: and yet thou never gavest me a kid, that I might make merry with my friends: But as soon as this thy son was come, which hath devoured thy living with harlots, thou hast killed for him the fatted calf. And he said unto him, Son, thou art ever with me, and all that I have is thine.

*It was meet that we should make merry, and be glad:
for this thy brother was dead, and is alive again; and
was lost, and is found.*

Another parable—Jesus' strongest, most poignant,
in my opinion—to show the true nature of the Father's
heart. He is not giving advice to earthly fathers as to
how to rear a son. And although there is much, much
here of spiritual help for those who have strayed away
from the Father's house, for purposes of symmetry and
clarity, we will look only at the marvelously balanced
structure of Luke's Chapter 15: from beginning to end,
a characterization of the *seeking, rejoicing* Father. The
ninety-nine sheep who remained in the shepherd's
fold could not argue that they had been neglected while
the shepherd hunted the one that was lost. Sheep can
neither argue nor complain. At least, not in language
to upset people. The nine remaining coins did not
show signs of jealousy because the woman swept her
house and searched until she found the lost coin. Coins
do not show signs. But the elder brother, in the third
parallel parable, flared at his father: "Look, how many
years have I slaved for you and never disobeyed a single
order of yours, and yet you have never given me so
much as a young goat, so that I could give my friends
a dinner! But when that son of yours arrives, who has
spent all your money on prostitutes, for *him* you kill
the calf we've fattened!" (Phillips). (Notice, when refer-
ring to the prodigal the elder brother did not call him
"my brother," but "your son.") Jesus' fictitious father in
the parable went right on acting and being like his

heavenly Father: "My dear son, you have been with me all the time and everything I have is yours. But we *had* to celebrate and show our joy. For this is your brother: I thought he was dead—and he's alive. I thought he was lost—and he is found." Is the Father really like this? Yes, he is. Or his own Son was wrong about him.

CHAPTER 16

vv. 24 through 26

And he cried and said, Father Abraham, have mercy on me, and send Lazarus, that he may dip the tip of his finger in water, and cool my tongue; for I am tormented in this flame. But Abraham said, Son, remember that thou in thy lifetime receivedst thy good things, and likewise Lazarus evil things: but now he is comforted, and thou art tormented. And beside all this, between us and you there is a great gulf fixed. . . .

Here we see the frightening consequence of man's steadfast refusal to consider the needs of his less fortunate fellow man. So locked was the heart of the rich man that he was unaware of the beggar, Lazarus, until Lazarus ended up at God's side and the rich man wallowed in the torment inevitable to the condition of his selfish heart. The difference between these two men was like a "great gulf fixed." And Jesus contended that nothing could have shaken the rich man from his self-love and indifference.

CHAPTER 17

vv. 5, 6

And the apostles said unto the Lord, Increase our faith. And the Lord said, If ye had faith as a grain of mustard seed, ye might say unto this sycamine tree, Be thou plucked up by the root, and be thou planted in the sea; and it should obey you.

It is not the amount of faith we have—even faith the minuscule size of a mustard seed will do. It's the object of our faith that matters. *Faith in God* can uproot things!

vv. 7 through 10

But which of you, having a servant plowing or feeding cattle, will say unto him by and by, when he is come from the field, Go and sit down to meat? And will not rather say unto him, Make ready wherewith I may sup, and gird thyself, and serve me, till I have eaten and drunken; and afterward thou shalt eat and drink? Doth he thank that servant because he did the things that were commanded him? I trow not. So likewise ye, when ye shall have done all those things which are commanded you, say, We are unprofitable servants: we have done that which was our duty to do.

This passage worried me for a long time. It seemed unlike the God of the parables of the lost sheep, the lost coin and the prodigal. Now, I see it only points up his grace! If this is the way we are, then isn't it all the more amazing that God could rejoice when an "unprofitable servant" comes home?

vv. 15, 16

And one of them, when he saw that he was healed, turned back, and with a loud voice glorified God, And fell down on his face at his feet, giving him thanks: and he was a Samaritan.

Luke must have had a special concern for race relations, for brotherhood. Have you noticed his tendency to point up the good characteristics of Samaritans? The other nine lepers seem to have been Jews. At least this is implied. Luke calls our attention to the fact that a hated Samaritan was the only one of the ten who bothered to say thank you to Jesus.

CHAPTER 18

vv. 1 through 7

And he spake a parable unto them to this end, that men ought always to pray, and not to faint; Saying, There was in a city a judge, which feared not God, neither regarded man: And there was a widow in that city; and she came unto him, saying, Avenge me of mine adversary. And he would not for a while: but afterward he said within himself, Though I fear not God, nor regard man; Yet because this widow troubleth me, I will avenge her, lest by her continual coming she weary me. And the Lord said, Hear what the unjust judge saith. And shall not God avenge his own elect, which cry day and night unto him, though he bear long with them?

Except for the three clear ones in Chapter 15, to me, most of the parables are difficult. So far, I find myself reading them often and swiftly, attempting an over-all impression—a spiritual "idea" of what he is saying. I don't think Jesus was deliberately obscure. Perhaps it is the "spiritual idea" he wants to convey. Here, what I see is that if man, temperamentally loath to do his duty, does it for a friendless widow just because she is persistent, how much more willing is God to listen to the petitions of his children? He speaks in these chapters of apocalyptic mysteries which could frighten us all. I make no attempt to deal with them, but I do see Jesus reassuring us steadily, by sandwiching in these marvelously quieting concepts of God. Because of what Jesus shows God to be like, I can relax about the things I do not understand.

vv. 10 through 14

Two men went up into the temple to pray; the one a Pharisee, and the other a publican. The Pharisee stood and prayed thus with himself, God, I thank thee, that I am not as other men are, extortioners, unjust, adulterers, or even as this publican. I fast twice in the week, I give tithes of all that I possess. And the publican, standing afar off, would not lift up so much as his eyes unto heaven, but smote upon his breast, saying, God be merciful to me a sinner. I tell you, this man went down to his house justified rather than the other: for every one that exalteth himself shall be abased; and he that humbleth himself shall be exalted.

One fresh insight comes to me here (at least for me it is fresh). So much has been written about the Pharisee and the publican, but what I'd like to add is that all that is required with God is honesty. The publican was honest. The Pharisee was not; either he was not or he had missed the point of humility before God for so long that he had lost sight of what honesty really is. Perhaps he was so neurotic that he really did feel himself better than the publican. I've known men like that. Women too. True honesty before God brings self-knowledge. And self-knowledge in the presence of God brings peace.

CHAPTER 19

vv. 5, 6 (Read vv. 1 through 10.)

And when Jesus came to the place, he looked up, and saw him, and said unto him, Zacchaeus, make haste, and come down; for to day I must abide at thy house. And he made haste, and came down, and received him joyfully.

I love Zacchaeus. Many people do. I think Luke liked him. But this was far from the case with Zacchaeus' neighbors and the people of Jericho who lived when he lived. They hated him because he was a rich publican. The publican's opportunities to assess great wealth were due to the unjust extortion possible under the system by which the collection of taxes was farmed out to individuals. Zacchaeus was utterly, selfishly practical. He looked out for Zacchaeus. Even to climbing the tree for a better look at Jesus when he passed by. But somewhere in this man was the potential for a true response to love. Jesus sensed it, looked up in the tree where Zacchaeus was perched, and called out to him: "Zacchaeus, make haste, and come down; for today I must abide at thy house!" The insignificant, hated little rich man scurried down out of the tree and "received him joyfully." And Zacchaeus' practical sense did not desert him: even his repentance was practical. He did not just say "I'm sorry, Lord. I'll do better." He laid it on the line: "Behold, Lord, the half of my goods I give to the poor; and if I have taken anything from any man by false accusation, I restore it to him fourfold." With a glad heart and no reservations, Jesus could reply: "This day is salvation come to this house, . . ." The

Saviour had come to save that which was lost. And Zacchaeus did not fool around. He was thoroughly lost, but then at the first glimpse of Jesus, he was thoroughly saved!

vv. 37 through 40

> *And when he was come nigh, even now at the descent of the mount of Olives, the whole multitude of the disciples began to rejoice and praise God with a loud voice for all the mighty works that they had seen; Saying, Blessed be the King that cometh in the name of the Lord: peace in heaven, and glory in the highest. And some of the Pharisees from among the multitude said unto him, Master, rebuke thy disciples. And he answered and said unto them, I tell you that, if these should hold their peace, the stones would immediately cry out.*

Jesus is entering Jerusalem at last, on the colt, as was prophesied. How closely God stayed with the established Jewish pattern. How he longed over his chosen people, doing all possible to enable them to feel at home in the revolutionary new kind of Kingdom his Son came proclaiming. And as Jesus rode toward the Holy City, "multitudes of his disciples began to rejoice and praise God with a loud voice for all the mighty works that they had seen." Most of them, perhaps all, did not realize toward what agony he was riding. They were filled with joy and they let it be known in no uncertain terms. They were rowdy—yelling and cheering—and it irked the frustrated Pharisees who had not yet trapped him, so they demanded that Jesus rebuke them for their uncouth behavior. He refused, knowing *where the disciples were* in their understanding. They just had to cheer what they had seen with their own eyes! There was no longer any point in repressing them. The forces against him were too strong to permit a bloody uprising. The time was too short. Let them cheer.

v. 41

And when he was come near, he beheld the city, and wept over it, . . .

He was near tears as they cheered, knowing what he knew—not about his sufferings ahead, but about the city he loved, the City of God, Jerusalem. There is a point on the road over the Mount of Olives where the city bursts into view. His disciples shouted and cheered, but "when he was come near, he beheld the city, and wept over it."

vv. 47, 48

And he taught daily in the temple. But the chief priests and the scribes and the chief of the people sought to destroy him, And could not find what they might do: for all the people were very attentive to hear him.

The chief priests and the scribes were "people pleasers" first. They were still after him, but they were hard put to it to find a way to destroy him without upsetting the people who were still "very attentive to hear him." Jesus knew this, and took full advantage of it.

CHAPTER 20

vv. 19 and 20

And the chief priests and the scribes the same hour sought to lay hands on him; and they feared the people: for they perceived that he had spoken this parable against them. And they watched him, and sent forth spies, which should feign themselves just men, that they might take hold of his words, that so they might deliver him unto the power and authority of the governor.

There could be no doubt even to the darkened minds of the chief priests and the scribes that Jesus directed this stinging parable about the absentee vineyard owner at them. Their only recourse was to double their efforts to trap him. To double their watch on him. To increase the number of spies who were to pass themselves off as "just men" so that they might "deliver him unto the power and authority of the governor." They were closing in on him swiftly, time ran short, the questions became more astute, trickier than ever before. In the presence of his majesty and dignity, the questions became more superificial *seeming*, but each one bore barbs to hook him, to force him to play into their determined hands.

vv. 45, 46, 47

Then in the audience of all the people he said unto his disciples, Beware of the scribes, which desire to walk in long robes, and love greetings in the markets, and the highest seats in the synagogues, and the chief rooms at feasts; Which devour widows' houses, and for a shew make long prayers: the same shall receive greater damnation.

He was walking steadfastly into their trap, but he was still their judge! They did not know it, but he was still, as he had been from the beginning, in charge of their souls.

CHAPTER 21
vv. 37, 38

And in the day time he was teaching in the temple; and at night he went out, and abode in the mount that is called the mount of Olives. And all the people came early in the morning to him in the temple, for to hear him.

From Sunday to Thursday of Holy Week, "in the day time he was [still] teaching in the temple. . . ." He would be about his father's business until the last minute. At night he went, presumably with his disciples, to the Mount of Olives to rest. But always, early the next day, the people were in the temple waiting for him to begin teaching again. And to the very last day, he was there.

CHAPTER 22
vv. 15 through 23

And he said unto them, With desire I have desired to eat this passover with you before I suffer: For I say unto you, I will not any more eat thereof, until it be fufilled in the kingdom of God. And he took the cup, and gave thanks, and said, Take this, and divide it among yourselves: For I say unto you, I will not drink of the fruit of the vine, until the kingdom of God shall come. And he took bread, and gave thanks, and brake it, and gave unto them, saying, This is my body which is given for

you: this do in remembrance of me. Likewise also the
cup after supper, saying, This cup is the new testament
in my blood, which is shed for you. But, behold, the
hand of him that betrayeth me is with me on the table.
And truly the Son of man goeth, as it was determined:
but woe unto that man by whom he is betrayed! And
they began to enquire among themselves, which of them
it was that should do this thing.

He "desired" to eat this last Passover feast with them
before he suffered. Judas had made his deal and Jesus
knew it because he knew Judas. He would not eat again
with them "until it be fulfilled in the kingdom of God."
Before the cup and the bread, he *gave thanks*. By all he
must suffer, he could be thankful because his act would
usher in the Kingdom on earth, and his beloved disciples would benefit. How he loved them. A "new testament"—a new covenant from God—was at hand. This
one eternal in the heavens and on the earth. He longed
to be remembered by them when they would again
repeat this supper after he was gone. And Judas was
still at the table! *He loved Judas, too.* (Luke does not
say Judas fled into the darkness, but, from the other
accounts, we know Judas left soon after this.)

v. 24

   And there was also a strife among them, which of
them should be accounted the greatest.

This is difficult to believe, but in the midst of this
deeply meaningful, sorrowful meal together, a wrangle
broke out on the same old note: Who is going to be the

greatest in the kingdom? It is obvious that none of the
men yet believed Jesus would go through with death.

vv. 31, 32

*And the Lord said, Simon, Simon, behold, Satan hath
desired to have you, that he may sift you as wheat: But
I have prayed for thee, that thy faith fail not: and when
thou art converted, strengthen thy brethren.*

In spite of their crassness, the Lord had messages of
love and caring for them. He knew the men had not
been truly converted to his way. Not yet. They loved
him as their Master, but even though he knew he had
influenced their thinking, a conversion that would last
would not be possible without the power of the Holy
Spirit within each man. *And Pentecost had not happened yet.* He must suffer first.

vv. 35 through 38

*And he said unto them, When I sent you without
purse, and scrip, and shoes, lacked ye any thing? And
they said, Nothing. Then said he unto them, But now,
he that hath a purse, let him take it, and likewise his
scrip: and he that hath no sword, let him sell his garment, and buy one. For I say unto you, that this that is
written must yet be accomplished in me, And he was
reckoned among the transgressors: for the things concerning me have an end. And they said, Lord, behold,
here are two swords. And he said unto them, It is enough.*

A warning to get ready for danger ahead. But *not* to
resist it by force. His words "It is enough" dismiss the
whole idea of resistance. Two swords for the whole
group would be enough to protect them against unex-

pected danger from wild animals, and so forth, but at the betrayal a short time later, Jesus made it plain that he did not operate by the sword.

vv. 50, 51

And one of them smote the servant of the high priest, and cut off his right ear. And Jesus answered and said, Suffer ye thus far. And he touched his ear, and healed him.

Jesus healed the damaged ear, saying: "That will do!" (Phillips). His was the way of peace, not the sword, where resistance was concerned. (John says it was Peter who drew his sword and cut off the servant, Malchus' ear.)

vv. 60, 61, 62

And Peter said, Man, I know not what thou sayest. And immediately, while he yet spake, the cock crew. And the Lord turned, and looked upon Peter. . . . And Peter went out, and wept bitterly.

When the rooster crowed, Peter was still in the process of denying Jesus for the third time. The words were not yet out of his mouth. The sound of the cock crowing must have been like a crash against his heart. And at the sound, Jesus, who was being led past him, bound with ropes, turned and *looked upon Peter.* He spoke no word of condemnation to his unstable disciple. *He just looked at him.* There was no need for words. That look did it. Peter went out and wept bitterly. Over his weeping, he could hear the sounds of the mockery and the spitting and the crack and slap of their hands as they struck his Master repeatedly in the face. He was out of Jesus' sight, but he would never forget that *look*.

CHAPTER 23

vv. 4 through 9

> *Then said Pilate to the chief priests and to the people, I find no fault in this man. And they were the more fierce, saying, He stirreth up the people, teaching throughout all Jewry, beginning from Galilee to this place. When Pilate heard of Galilee, he asked whether the man were a Galilaean. And as soon as he knew that he belonged unto Herod's jurisdiction, he sent him to Herod, who himself also was at Jerusalem at that time. And when Herod saw Jesus, he was exceeding glad: for he was desirous to see him of a long season, because he had heard many things of him; and he hoped to have seen some miracle done by him. Then he questioned with him in many words; but he answered him nothing.*

Jesus stands, a moral, mental and spiritual giant alongside Pilate and Herod. He dwarfs them in every way, showing Pilate as evasive and cowardly; Herod as downright silly, wanting to be entertained, hoping to see him perform a miracle!

v. 27

> *And there followed him a great company of people, and of women, which also bewailed and lamented him.*

Only Luke mentions that the women who loved him walked the Via Dolorosa with him as he stumbled toward Calvary.

vv. 28 through 31

But Jesus turning unto them said, Daughters of Jerusalem, weep not for me, but weep for yourselves, and for your children. For, behold, the days are coming, in the which they shall say, Blessed are the barren, and the wombs that never bare, and the paps which never gave suck. Then shall they begin to say to the mountains, Fall on us; and to the hills, Cover us. For if they do these things in a green tree, what shall be done in the dry?

And as always, even on this last torturous walk, he was teaching and warning.

vv. 32 through 34

And there were also two other, malefactors, led with him to be put to death. And when they were come to the place, which is called Calvary, there they crucified him, and the malefactors, one on the right hand, and the other on the left. Then said Jesus, Father, forgive them; for they know not what they do. And they parted his raiment, and cast lots.

Two criminals went with him to their deaths, one hung on his right hand and one on his left. At this point perhaps the one criminal was silent, except for sharp cries of pain as the nails pierced his flesh and the long cry of unbelief at the amount of total pain when the weight of his body sagged against the nails. The other criminal hung there cursing and railing—not at his crucifiers, but at Jesus.

Jesus was praying for the forgiveness of his tormentors, and a manifestation of love like this evokes either curses or submission.

v. 35

And the people stood beholding. And the rulers also with them derided him, saying, He saved others; let him save himself, if he be Christ, the chosen of God.

His old antagonists, the rulers, were there too, enjoying their "victory" to the end. Still heckling him.

vv. 39 through 43

And one of the malefactors which were hanged railed on him, saying, If thou be Christ, save thyself and us. But the other answering rebuked him, saying, Dost not thou fear God, seeing thou art in the same condemnation? And we indeed justly; for we receive the due reward of our deeds: but this man hath done nothing amiss. And he said unto Jesus, Lord, remember me when thou comest into thy kingdom. And Jesus said unto him, Verily I say unto thee, To day shalt thou be with me in paradise.

The repentant thief followed no ritual, received no baptism, became a member of no church, memorized no Scripture verses, kept no regular quiet times. He just turned to Jesus with an open, contrite heart and asked to be remembered. Jesus' forgiving spirit, even on his Cross, had won the criminal's heart.

CHAPTER 24

vv. 6 through 12

He is not here, but is risen: remember how he spake unto you when he was yet in Galilee, Saying, The Son of man must be delivered into the hands of sinful men, and be crucified, and the third day rise again. And they remembered his words, And returned from the sepulchre, and told all these things unto the eleven, and to

*all the rest. It was Mary Magdalene, and Joanna, and
Mary the mother of James, and other women that were
with them, which told these things unto the apostles.
And their words seemed to them as idle tales, and they
believed them not. Then arose Peter, and ran unto the
sepulchre; and stooping down, he beheld the linen
clothes laid by themselves, and departed, wondering in
himself at that which was come to pass.*

Luke reports two angels at the empty tomb. No
matter the number. What they said to the grieving
women is the important thing: "Why seek ye the living
among the dead?" And then they reminded Mary of
Magdala and Mary, the mother of James, and their
friends that Jesus had told them he would be crucified
and that on the third day he would rise again. With this
prod from the angels, they remembered his words! Suddenly it was all making sense to them, and they ran to
tell the eleven remaining disciples. Only Peter gave
enough credence to their "idle tales" to run to the tomb
to see for himself. (John writes that he ran with them,
but Luke does not report this.) Peter seems still a touch
skeptical. Unlike the women who believed, he merely
wonders. Did the disciples' egos block their believing?
After all, *they* were the men whom he had chosen by
name to be his intimates. The women had followed
Jesus of their own accord, out of gratitude for what he
had done for them. There is no record that he cast any
devils out of Peter or James or John or any of the
Twelve. He chose them, and in their still unregenerate
states, this must have gone to their heads.

vv. 13 through 26

And, behold, two of them went that same day to a village called Emmaus, which was from Jerusalem about threescore furlongs. And they talked together of all these things which had happened. And it came to pass, that, while they communed together and reasoned, Jesus himself drew near, and went with them. But their eyes were holden that they should not know him. And he said unto them, What manner of communications are these that ye have one to another, as ye walk, and are sad? And the one of them, whose name was Cleopas, answering said unto him, Art thou only a stranger in Jerusalem, and hast not known the things which are come to pass there in these days? And he said unto them, What things? And they said unto him, Concerning Jesus of Nazareth, which was a prophet mighty in deed and word before God and all the people: And how the chief priests and our rulers delivered him to be condemned to death, and have crucified him. But we trusted that it had been he which should have redeemed Israel: and beside all this, to day is the third day since these things were done. Yea, and certain women also of our company made us astonished, which were early at the sepulchre; And when they found not his body, they came, saying, that they had also seen a vision of angels, which said that he was alive. And certain of them which were with us went to the sepulchre, and found it even so as the women had said: but him they saw not. Then he said unto them, O fools, and slow of heart to believe all that the prophets have spoken: Ought not Christ to have suffered these things, and to enter into his glory?

These two disciples were not of the original Twelve, but evidently, they were close, and present with the others, when the women came to tell them the Lord was risen. Their horror at what had happened to him must have blinded their eyes. This and their own personal disappointment that they would not be among his intimates when he set up his kingdom. They could never be now. Their king had gone down to defeat. These few facts robbed them of their "little faith." Peter and John had not actually seen Jesus when they ran to the Sepulcher to check out the women's story, and the men had all accepted the fact of defeat.

In verse 26 Jesus said a most revealing thing to them: "Ought not Christ to have suffered these things . . . ?" To me, that is one of the most poignant and truest characterizations of God! Wasn't he saying: "Could I, the Son of the God who loves all of you so much, do *any less* than I did?"

vv. 27 through 32

And beginning at Moses and all the prophets, he expounded unto them in all the scriptures the things concerning himself. And they drew nigh unto the village, whither they went: and he made as though he would have gone further. But they constrained him, saying, Abide with us: for it is toward evening, and the day is far spent. And he went in to tarry with them. And it came to pass, as he sat at meat with them, he took bread, and blessed it, and brake, and gave to them. And their eyes were opened, and they knew him; and he vanished out of their sight. And they said one to another, Did not our heart burn within us, while he talked with us by the way, and while he opened to us the scriptures?

The disciples en route to Emmaus were not of the Twelve, but they had heard in detail of how he broke bread during the Last Supper and called it his body that would be broken for them. When he took the bread that night at dinner with them, and blessed it and broke it—they knew him. That was all he was after—*recognition*. Once they recognized him as their Lord, he vanished. Their hearts had burned within them as he opened the Scriptures on the way to Emmaus, but evidently that was not enough to cause them to know him. The broken bread did it.

vv. 33 through 43

And they rose up the same hour, and returned to Jerusalem, and found the eleven gathered together, and them that were with them, Saying, The Lord is risen indeed, and hath appeared to Simon. And they told what things were done in the way, and how he was known of them in breaking of bread. And as they thus spake, Jesus himself stood in the midst of them, and saith unto them, Peace be unto you. But they were terrified and affrighted, and supposed that they had seen a spirit. And he said unto them, Why are ye troubled? and why do thoughts arise in your hearts? Behold my hands and my feet, that it is I myself: handle me, and see; for a spirit hath not flesh and bones, as ye see me have. And when he had thus spoken, he shewed them his hands and his feet. And while they yet believed not for joy, and wondered, he said unto them, Have ye here any meat? And they gave him a piece of a broiled fish, and of an honeycomb. And he took it, and did eat before them.

Now, they were excited and hurried back to find the other men. Together again, they all began comparing stories, wondering, analyzing, theorizing. And as they talked, Jesus himself stood there among them and said: "Peace be unto you." And once more, he did all he could do to dispel their doubts. Specifically, he ate something. Would a mere spirit eat food?

v. 45

Then opened he their understanding, that they might understand the scriptures,

I have always been struck with the mystery of this verse. How did he open their understanding? It is not for us to know; at least, it is not vital that we know. But we can suppose he did it as he does it now with us —through the Holy Spirit. For that brief time with him, they must somehow have had access to the Spirit from within, as they all had after Pentecost. As we all have now.

vv. 49 through 53

And, behold, I send the promise of my Father upon you: but tarry ye in the city of Jerusalem, until ye be endued with power from on high. And he led them out as far as to Bethany, and he lifted up his hands, and blessed them. And it came to pass, while he blessed them, he was parted from them, and carried up into heaven. And they worshipped him, and returned to Jerusalem with great joy: And were continually in the temple, praising and blessing God. Amen.

Luke ends his Gospel on a continuing note. The end of the written account is in truth, a beginning. Since Luke is also the writer of Acts, he has made the link here. Jesus promises them they will be "endued with power from on high" if they will follow his instructions and tarry in Jerusalem—together. And leaving them, he led them out as far as their old familiar resting place at Bethany. He led them and blessed them and as he was blessing them, his hands lifted up, he was parted from them—back to his Father in heaven.

The disciples did not weep and wail and shout for his return. "They worshipped him, and returned to Jerusalem with great joy . . ."! And were continually in the temple, after that, praising God and rejoicing, their expectations high.

SAINT JOHN

CHAPTER 1
vv. 1, 2

In the beginning was the Word, and the Word was with God, and the Word was God. The same was in the beginning with God.

There is light from many of the newer translations on these first two verses, but none equals the King James version in pure poetry. I am convinced no one will ever write a more perfect sentence than the sentence we know as the first verse of this Gospel. The second verse emphasizes what has already been almost perfectly said, and to me, this is the key to John's entire Gospel: He wants it made very, very clear at the outset that *Jesus Christ is central.* That He is not, in any way, less than God himself. There was Someone else there with the Father "in the beginning." The first verse of the Gospel of John linked with verse 26 of the first chapter of Genesis makes a totally believable whole. Look at them together:

"In the beginning was the Word, and the Word was with God, and the word was God" (John 1:1).

"And God said, Let *us* make man in our image, after *our* likeness" (Genesis 1:26). (Author's italics.)

The two verses could have been written by the same person as far as the literary beauty and simplicity and phrasing go. And to me, they are marvelously melded in meaning. They do not explain redemption, but they put God within reach by making it clear that there *was* Someone else there "in the beginning" who could come to us in Person. Someone equal with God, the Creator.

v. 3

All things were made by him: and without him was not any thing made that was made.

The poetry still stands up here: "All things were made by him: and without him was not any thing made that was made." There will never be a more musical sentence. But most important, we are permitted, right at the very beginning of John's account, to rest everything we are on the *fact* that this Man about whom he will be writing was *not* just another great teacher. He was not only "with God," he *was* God. And, what's more, he was the Creator God: ". . . without him was not any thing made that was made." Whatever this God-Man had to say was *truth*. Not because of his undeniably superior intellect, but because of *who he was!* John writes from the standpoint of Hebrew philosophy, beginning with the fact of God. With the Hebrew mind there was no need to prove God, as with the Greek mind. One either believes or does not believe in a

Supreme Being of some kind. John's purpose is not to prove God. He begins with that premise as established. His purpose *is to make it as clear as possible that God revealed himself as he really is in Jesus of Nazareth.*

vv. 4, 5

In him was life; and the life was the light of men. And the light shineth in darkness; and the darkness comprehended it not.

The poetry goes on as John equates life with light. There is no possible way to experience entire truth without this "life" within us. Half-truth, yes. Great learning, yes. But not entire truth. This life of Christ "still shines in the darkness and the darkness has never put it out" (Phillips). It can never be put out. John is offering absolute assurance: There is the fact of God, the fact of Christ, and the fact of the light he brings which no amount of human darkness can extinguish.

vv. 6 through 18

There was a man sent from God, whose name was John. The same came for a witness, to bear witness of the Light, that all men through him might believe. He was not that Light, but was sent to bear witness of that Light. That was the true Light, which lighteth every man that cometh into the world. He was in the world, and the world was made by him, and the world knew him not. He came unto his own, and his own received him not. But as many as received him, to them gave he power to become the sons of God, even to them that believe on his name: Which were born, not of blood, nor of the will of the flesh, nor of the will of man, but of God. And the Word was made flesh, and dwelt among us, (and we beheld his glory, the glory as of the only begotten of the Father,) full of grace and truth. John bare witness of him, and cried, saying, This was he of whom I spake, He that cometh after me is preferred before me: for he was before me. And of his fulness have all we received, and grace for grace. For the law was given by Moses, but grace and truth came by Jesus Christ. No man hath seen God at any time; the only begotten Son, which is in the bosom of the Father, he hath declared him.

Before John tells the story of the ministry of John the Baptist, he nails down his premise of truth with long, shining nails. There was a man named John who came announcing the Light, but John was not the Light. The world did not recogize this Light, the One who *was* this Light, but he was already in the world—the Son of God *had come.* And everyone who did recognize him was enabled to become a son of God also. Far-fetched? John doesn't mind that. He is declaring truth and truth will defend itself. Truth will defend *Himself.* And in verse 14 (which to me could follow 1 and 2 with perfect continuity) he tells us *who this was* who was with God in the beginning. He identifies that Word who "was with God"—"who *was* God." It would seem John had reached his crescendo when he declares: "And the Word was made flesh, and dwelt among us, (and we beheld his glory, the glory as of the only begotten of the Father,) full of grace and truth." Whoever this was with God in the beginning had come to earth to live among us! And he was full not only of grace, but of truth. "And we beheld his glory, . . ." John, the writer, *saw* him. John the Baptist was proclaiming him to be "before him" because he *was* "in the beginning" with God. It seems as though John, the author of the Gospel, is unable for a little while longer to launch into the actual narrative. "One more thing, I must tell you," he appears to be saying, "and that is that 'no man hath seen God at any time, but the only begotten Son . . . (this Jesus of Nazareth, my Master), *he hath declared him*'!" Another crescendo following a crescendo. There is no limit to them for John. He has *seen* Truth Himself—all the high barred gates have been flung open! The mounting crescendos can go on and on now, through eternity. His Master, Jesus Christ, has come to make God known to all men. Moses brought the law, but Christ has come to make it possible—by the very grace he brings—to keep that law. The lowliest man or woman can now *know* the God of Israel! Can know his intentions toward us, can know his heart, can begin to understand his ways.

v. 29

The next day John seeth Jesus coming unto him, and saith, Behold the Lamb of God, which taketh away the sin of the world.

The climactic moment of the lonely, isolated, wholly dedicated life of Elisabeth's son, John, has come. He sees Jesus walking toward him through the crowd, and shouts: "Behold the Lamb of God, which taketh away the sin of the world"! No more need for sacrificial lambs on the altar of the Lord. Jesus has come; he who *has been* the sacrificial lamb since the foundation of the world. He who has been ". . . slain from the foundation of the world" (Revelations 13:8). It has all been in God's plan from the beginning. The sin of mankind came as no surprise to the Lord God. When he created, he already had redemption under way!

vv. 35 through 37

> *Again the next day after John stood, and two of his disciples; And looking upon Jesus as he walked, he saith, Behold the Lamb of God! And the two disciples heard him speak, and they followed Jesus.*

Talking with two of his own disciples, John the Baptist, ". . . looking upon Jesus as he walked, . . . saith, Behold the Lamb of God!" Repeating himself for the sake of his own disciples, wanting so much for them to know the truth of what he had been telling them about the One who would come to save Israel from her sins. Wanting to impress upon them that he, their master, John, was *not* the Messiah, but that the Messiah, Jesus, was now among them. In those days, a teacher's reputation was mainly dependent upon the *loyalty* of the men who followed him. John risked this, so convinced was he of the *truth* God had taught him during those years alone in the wilderness. In verse 37, we see that John's two disciples left him to follow Jesus. Humanly speaking, this would be hard for a man to take. With John the Baptist, it meant he had taught his disciples well. They "heard him speak," they got his message and followed *Jesus.*

vv. 45 through 50

Philip findeth Nathanael, and saith unto him, We have found him, of whom Moses in the law, and the prophets, did write, Jesus of Nazareth, the son of Joseph. And Nathanael said unto him, Can there any good thing come out of Nazareth? Philip saith unto him, Come and see. Jesus saw Nathanael coming to him, and saith of him, Behold an Israelite indeed, in whom is no guile! Nathanael saith unto him, Whence knowest thou me? Jesus answered and said unto him, Before that Philip called thee, when thou wast under the fig tree, I saw thee. Nathanael answered and saith unto him, Rabbi, thou art the Son of God; thou art the King of Israel. Jesus answered, and said unto him, Because I said unto thee, I saw thee under the fig tree, believest thou? thou shalt see greater things than these.

John, the evangelist, writes of one provocative incident when Jesus is calling his disciples not mentioned in the other three Gospel accounts. The men are excited: Andrew ran to call his brother, Simon; Philip ran to call his friend, Nathanael. And when he learned from Philip that he had found "him of whom Moses in the law, and the prophets, did write" and that he was Jesus of Nazareth, the son of Joseph, Nathanael made what can be interpreted as a smart-alecky, sarcastic remark: "Can there any good thing come out of Nazareth?" In fact, this has, with usage, become a sarcastic question. Or perhaps it was considered so then. Still, Jesus said of

Nathanael, "Behold an Israelite indeed in whom is no guile!" Nathanael's question did not sound one bit guileless. *But Jesus knew Nathanael.* The Master never acted or reacted on mere words. Always he looked beneath the words at the man. Evidently Nathanael *was* guileless. Nazareth was an obscure little hill country town. No one of any note had ever come from there. To me, Nathanael was simply asking a natural question.

In verses 49 and 50, we need to think ahead to Peter's declaration that Jesus was the Christ, the Son of God. Why is that given more importance—treated usually, as the first time any man really had the Lord's identity straight? It occurs to me that because of what Jesus replied to Nathanael when he declared him right away to be the Son of God, the King of Israel, that Jesus here is merely letting it be known that he *does* see into not only the heart, but the intelligence and judgment of a man. Obviously, he knew that his new disciple, Nathanael, was not only guileless, but impulsive. Jesus recommended that Nathanael wait a while and really see what was up ahead before jumping to conclusions concerning the Master's identity. The Lord is always interested in our believing with our *whole* hearts.

CHAPTER 2

vv. 8 through 11

And he saith unto them, Draw out now, and bear unto the governor of the feast. And they bare it. When the ruler of the feast had tasted the water that was made wine, and knew not whence it was: (but the servants which drew the water knew;) the governor of the feast called the bridegroom, And saith unto him, Every man at the beginning doth set forth good wine; and when men have well drunk, then that which is worse: but thou hast kept the good wine until now. This beginning of miracles did Jesus in Cana of Galilee, and manifested forth his glory; and his disciples believed on him.

The wine episode at the marriage feast in Cana has caused no end of confusion. That Jesus turned the water into wine is fact, and John emphasizes it. I think it is intended to be neither an aid nor a stumbling block for those who choose to fight the liquor interests. There is nothing so superficial here. I do not suggest that I understand all there is to understand about the use of this incident, but it is the first recorded miracle of Jesus in John and it should not be dodged. Troubling questions arise: Was it worthy of the Son of God that his first miracle should be the mere relieving of a social embarrassment at a wedding feast? Does it jibe with his usual reluctance to work miracles for the sake of working miracles? Was it sensible to have made *so much* wine? More than one hundred gallons? I don't think John invented the whole episode. I believe it happened as he told it. John was there. For me, the story has these values: It clearly demonstrates the difference between the attitude toward life Jesus held and the attitude toward life which John the Baptist held. Jesus' is the New Testament view, John's the Old. From this incident, we see that Jesus had come to mingle with men and women in the daily round, the ordinary events of their lives. It shows me in a remarkable way the gracious condescension of the Son of God. It is also true that in the Old Testament, wine symbolizes reconciliation with God (Isaiah 55:1): "Ho, everyone that thirsteth, come ye to the waters, and he that hath no money; come ye, buy and eat; yea, come, buy wine and milk without money and without price." And Isaiah 25:6: "And in this mountain shall the Lord of hosts make unto all people a feast of fat things, a feast of wines on the lees, . . ." Clearly, Isaiah is intimating the coming of a New Order. The New Order came with Jesus, and so the symbol of wine would have had definite spiritual meaning for the Jews at the wedding feast. It could well have been regarded as a sign that the Kingdom of God had come in the Person and activity of Jesus. I cannot help thinking too, of Jesus' use of wine as the symbol of his own blood to be shed. The time was coming, even though this miracle took place at the outset of his ministry, when Christ's atoning death would replace the ancient Jewish rites. The water of Judaism had been replaced by the wine of the Gospel. And perhaps he made such a quantity of wine to show us that with him no one was ever going to be stinted! Jesus came to give *abundance.*

v. 15

> *And when he had made a scourge of small cords, he drove them all out of the temple, and the sheep, and the oxen; and poured out the changers' money, and overthrew the tables; . . .*

I don't even try to understand this incident in relation to human anger. It wasn't. It was perhaps the only true righteous indignation ever experienced on the earth. The point is not whether it is "kind" to do what Jesus did. We need make no apologies. We need only to *try* to see at least dimly, how man's desecration of the holy affects God.

CHAPTER 3

vv. 1 through 3

There was a man of the Pharisees, named Nicodemus, a ruler of the Jews: The same came to Jesus by night, and said unto him, Rabbi, we know that thou art a teacher come from God: for no man can do these miracles that thou doest, except God be with him. Jesus answered and said unto him, Verily, verily, I say unto thee, Except a man be born again, he cannot see the kingdom of God.

The learned man, Nicodemus, was all set to have a profound theological discussion with Jesus as one rabbi to another. Jesus made anything resembling a merely academic conversation impossible by stating flatly, at the outset of their talk, that until a man is born all over again, he cannot even *see* the Kingdom of God!

v. 8

The wind bloweth where it listeth, and thou hearest the sound thereof, but canst not tell whence it cometh, and whither it goeth: so is every one that is born of the Spirit.

As I write, the tassels of Spanish moss on the live oaks outside my room are hanging straight and motionless. There is no perceptible sign of any wind stirring. Half an hour ago, the moss was whipping wildly in a high wind off the ocean as the tide changed. Now, these few lines later, I can see one and then two strands of gray moss move, hang limp a moment, then move again. We can only tell the wind is blowing by the movement we see in its path. *There are no pat answers in the Kingdom of God.*

vv. 16, 17

> *For God so loved the world, that he gave his only begotten Son, that whosoever believeth in him should not perish, but have everlasting life. For God sent not his Son into the world to condemn the world; but that the world through him might be saved.*

Dr. E. Stanley Jones called John 3:16: "The twenty-five most important words in history." They are. But I am seeing that we need verse 17 for clarity, for verification of verse 16. How far away we have wandered when our "religion" tends to cause us to look for faults, to condemn. Jesus reminded us constantly that the Son of God came, not to condemn the world, but to save it. Love never condemns. It does not merely condone, either. It *saves.*

vv. 18, 19

> *He that believeth on him is not condemned: but he that believeth not is condemned already, because he hath not believed in the name of the only begotten Son of*

*God. And this is the condemnation, that light is come
into the world, and men loved darkness rather than light,
because their deeds were evil.*

Man has already condemned himself by choosing
darkness. He needs no further condemnation, but he
does need saving love.

v. 35

*The Father loveth the Son, and hath given all things
into his hand.*

This truth is the greatest relief I know.

CHAPTER 4
v. 4

And he must needs go through Samaria.

It is as though he had no choice. There was so much
to teach *us* by going through Samaria.

vv. 6 through 8

*Now Jacob's well was there. Jesus therefore, being
wearied with his journey, sat thus on the well: and it
was about the sixth hour. There cometh a woman of
Samaria to draw water: Jesus saith unto her, Give me to
drink. (For his disciples were gone away unto the city
to buy meat.)*

Jesus met the woman alone. His disciples had gone
shopping. It is just as well. They could never have
done what he did: place himself in the position of
having to ask this outcast woman for a favor. "Please
give me a drink" (Phillips).

v. 9

Then saith the woman of Samaria unto him, How is it that thou, being a Jew, askest drink of me, which am a woman of Samaria? for the Jews have no dealings with the Samaritans.

I don't think the Samaritan woman was dodging any issues yet. She was simply a woman who came right out and said what she thought, and it was unheard of for a Jew to ask a favor of or even to speak to a Samaritan. Our race barriers pale by comparison.

v. 10

Jesus answered and said unto her, If thou knewest the gift of God, and who it is that saith to thee, Give me to drink; thou wouldest have asked of him, and he would have given thee living water.

As always, Jesus took advantage of every opening to prick the interest.

v. 11

The woman saith unto him, Sir, thou hast nothing to draw with, and the well is deep: from whence then hast thou that living water?

She may be hedging a bit here, but I don't think so. Plainly, he had no bucket. How could he possibly give her living water? Remember, this woman was—like too many people—a literalist.

v. 12

Art thou greater than our father Jacob, which gave us the well, and drank thereof himself, and his children, and his cattle?

She is sarcastic here, growing a touch uneasy.

vv. 13 through 15

Jesus answered and said unto her, Whosoever drinketh of this water shall thirst again: But whosoever drinketh of the water that I shall give him shall never thirst; but the water that I shall give him shall be in him a well of water springing up into everlasting life. The woman saith unto him, Sir, give me this water, that I thirst not, neither come hither to draw.

She grabbed at his offer, but he did not settle for her impulsive request for the living water he spoke of. He knew her motives were mixed. After all, she came regularly to the well at a time of day when the other women were *not* there. She had the kind of reputation that forces a woman to avoid other women when possible. And *if* this strange Man could give her water that would so satisfy her thirst she would never have to come to the well again, it would be fine.

vv. 16 through 24

Jesus saith unto her, Go, call thy husband, and come hither. The woman answered and said, I have no husband. Jesus said unto her, Thou hast well said, I have no husband: For thou hast had five husbands; and he whom thou now hast is not thy husband: in that saidst thou truly. The woman saith unto him, Sir, I perceive that thou art a prophet. Our fathers worshipped in this mountain; and ye say, that in Jerusalem is the place where men ought to worship. Jesus saith unto her, Woman, believe me, the hour cometh, when ye shall neither in this mountain, nor yet at Jerusalem, worship the Father. Ye worship ye know not what: we know what we worship: for salvation is of the Jews. But the hour cometh, and now is, when the true worshippers shall worship the Father in spirit and in truth: for the Father seeketh such to worship him. God is a Spirit: and they that worship him must worship him in spirit and in truth.

His abrupt change of subject must have startled the woman. Suddenly, he was hitting a nerve. He shocked her, caught her off guard, so that she blurted out the truth to him. And he must have seen her long subdued conscience, still alive and able to feel guilt—thereby able to receive help. But there was that one moment of openness, and then her defenses flew back up, as she parried: " 'I can see that you're a prophet! Now our ancestors worshipped on this hillside, but you Jews say that Jerusalem is the place where men ought to worship—' " (Phillips translates this as a broken speech, with Jesus interrupting her.) " 'Believe me,' returned Jesus, 'the time is coming when worshipping the Father will not be a matter of "on this hillside" or "in Jerusalem" . . . God is Spirit, and those who worship him can only worship in spirit and in reality' " (Phillips). It must have "gotten to her"; perhaps she felt included for the first time, when Jesus told her the Father was seeking those who would be willing to worship him freely in spirit and reality—*truth.*

v. 25

> *The woman saith unto him, I know that Messias cometh, which is called Christ: when he is come, he will tell us all things.*

He touched a responsive place in her because immediately she mentioned the coming of the Messiah.

vv. 26 through 29

> *Jesus saith unto her, I that speak unto thee am he. And upon this came his disciples, and marvelled that he talked with the woman: yet no man said, What seekest thou? or, Why talkest thou with her? The woman then left her waterpot, and went her way into the city, and saith to the men, Come, see a man, which told me all things that ever I did: is not this the Christ?*

His simple, profound reply is the only place in the New Testament to my knowledge where—in so many exact words—he says he is the Christ. Immediately, the sinful woman—the last person on earth the religionists would select to be an evangel—ran to tell that she had met the Messiah! Her light was pale; she believed in him only because he had told her about herself, *but she believed.*

vv. 39 through 41

> *And many of the Samaritans of that city believed on him for the saying of the woman, which testified, He told me all that ever I did. So when the Samaritans were come unto him, they besought him that he would tarry with them: and he abode there two days. And many more believed because of his own word; . . .*

And many Samaritans believed because of her. The race barriers even went down so that they invited Jesus and his men—Jews—to stay two days with them! As with Mary of Magdala and the prodigal and all of us who know the immensity of our need, this woman's word held added weight. And once more there was rejoicing in heaven because a few more lost sheep came home. "Christ Jesus came into this world to *save* sinners. . . ." Not to condemn.

CHAPTER 5

v. 18

Therefore the Jews sought the more to kill him, because he not only had broken the sabbath, but said also that God was his Father, making himself equal with God.

What really stirred the Pharisees to fury was this hill-country itinerant preacher who dared to make himself equal with the God of Israel. Their conditioning had blinded their minds to receive any *new truth* about the God of their father Abraham. Sound familiar?

v. 22

For the Father judgeth no man, but hath committed all judgment unto the Son:

The Great Relief again. And how it must have rocked the learned Jews! This "upstart" would be sitting in judgment upon *them?* To their ears, blasphemy, pure and simple. His pomposity must be brought to an end by any available means.

CHAPTER 6

vv. 14, 15

Then those men, when they had seen the miracle that Jesus did, said, This is of a truth that prophet that should come into the world. When Jesus therefore perceived that they would come and take him by force, to make him a king, he departed again into a mountain himself alone.

When Jesus fed the multitude on this occasion, John tells us that the crowd went wild. Not in so many words are we told, but he tells us by way of Jesus' decision: "Then Jesus, realizing that they were going to carry him off and make him their king, retired once more to the hillside quite alone" (Phillips). His time had not yet come. *And* an earthly kingdom was *not* his purpose.

vv. 24 through 26

When the people therefore saw that Jesus was not there, neither his disciples, they also took shipping, and came to Capernaum, seeking for Jesus. And when they had found him on the other side of the sea, they said unto him, Rabbi, when camest thou hither? Jesus answered them and said, Verily, verily, I say unto you, Ye seek me, not because ye saw the miracles, but because ye did eat of the loaves, and were filled.

The people were determined to get at him. They followed him on foot and in boats. But (verse 26) he knew their motives were mixed. They didn't want him for himself, they wanted him for what he could do for them.

vv. 32 through 35, 41

Then Jesus said unto them, Verily, verily, I say unto you, Moses gave you not that bread from heaven; but my Father giveth you the true bread from heaven. For the bread of God is he which cometh down from heaven, and giveth life unto the world. Then said they unto him, Lord, evermore give us this bread. And Jesus said unto them, I am the bread of life: he that cometh to me shall never hunger; and he that believeth on me shall never thirst. . . . The Jews then murmured at him, because he said I am the bread which came down from heaven.

They taunted him with Moses and the manna, and when he declared himself to be the bread of life, their fury grew. They did not want *him*. He did not fit their concept of a God who doled out to his people in a material sense.

vv. 48 through 52

I am that bread of life. Your fathers did eat manna in the wilderness, and are dead. This is the bread which cometh down from heaven, that a man may eat thereof, and not die. I am the living bread which came down from heaven: if any man eat of this bread, he shall live for ever: and the bread that I will give is my flesh, which I will give for the life of the world. The Jews therefore strove among themselves, saying, How can this man give us his flesh to eat?

His words were spirit and their questions were all materialistic!

vv. 53 through 61

Then Jesus said unto them, Verily, verily, I say unto you, Except ye eat the flesh of the Son of man, and drink

*his blood, ye have no life in you. Whoso eateth my flesh,
and drinketh my blood, hath eternal life; and I will raise
him up at the last day. For my flesh is meat indeed, and
my blood is drink indeed. He that eateth my flesh, and
drinketh my blood, dwelleth in me, and I in him. As the
living Father hath sent me, and I live by the Father: so
he that eateth me, even he shall live by me. This is that
bread which came down from heaven: not as your fathers
did eat manna, and are dead: he that eateth of this bread
shall live for ever. These things said he in the synagogue,
as he taught in Capernaum. Many therefore of his
disciples, when they had heard this, said, This is an hard
saying; who can hear it? When Jesus knew in himself
that his disciples murmured at it, he said unto them,
Doth this offend you?*

He was not even slowed down by their anger. One
can feel the tension and tenderness and determination
in his voice when he repeatedly called himself the
bread of life. He was using a symbol common to everyone—everyone likes bread in some form. It is needed
for life. And yet they, even some of his disciples, were
so earth-bound and materialistic, they missed his point
entirely.

vv. 65 through 69

*And he said, Therefore said I unto you, that no man
can come unto me, except it were given unto him of my
Father. From that time many of his disciples went back,
and walked no more with him. Then said Jesus unto the
twelve, Will ye also go away? Then Simon Peter
answered him, Lord, to whom shall we go? thou hast
the words of eternal life. And we believe and are sure
that thou art that Christ, the Son of the living God.*

Some of his own turned and left him. And Jesus faced the Twelve asking, perhaps wearily: "Will ye also go away?" And Peter spoke a marvelous truth: "Lord, to whom shall we go?" Being with Jesus had spoiled everything else for Peter. The Twelve had come this far. They would stay with him.

Chapter 7

vv. 31, 32

And many of the people believed on him, and said, When Christ cometh, will he do more miracles than these which this man hath done? The Pharisees heard that the people murmured such things concerning him; ind the Pharisees and the chief priests sent officers to take him.

Then, as now, the people were in varying stages of belief. Some "believed on him" and expressed their belief this way: "When Christ cometh, will he do more miracles than these which this man hath done?" They did not yet have insight or courage to call *him* the Christ, but they were on their way. And the scribes and Pharisees grew more furious, more determined to kill him.

vv. 33, 34

Then said Jesus unto them, Yet a little while am I with you, and then I go unto him that sent me. Ye shall seek me, and shall not find me: and where I am, thither ye cannot come.

Jesus knew well what lay ahead. He had told his disciples repeatedly that he would be killed and now he said it to the people in their varying stages of belief, giving them warning also.

vv. 37, 38

In the last day, that great day of the feast, Jesus stood and cried, saying, If any man thirst, let him come unto me, and drink. He that believeth on me, as the scripture hath said, out of his belly shall flow rivers of living water.

Jesus made no effort to hide from his tormentors. At the feast of the Passover, with thousands to hear, "Jesus stood and *cried*, saying, if any man thirst, let him come unto me, and drink." His one burning passion was not to protect himself, but to make men hear and understand and follow him.

v. 39

(But this spake he of the Spirit, which they that believe on him should receive: for the Holy Ghost was not yet given; because that Jesus was not yet glorified.)

John, the author of this Gospel, here offers one of his several interpretative kindnesses. He explains that Jesus spoke of the Holy Spirit in v. 38, and that the Holy Spirit had not yet been given. As from the beginning of his account, John, too, longs for *our* understanding.

CHAPTER 8

vv. 3 through 6, 10, 11

And the scribes and Pharisees brought unto him a woman taken in adultery; and when they had set her in the midst, They say unto him, Master, this woman was taken in adultery, in the very act. Now Moses in the law commanded us, that such should be stoned: but what sayest thou? This they said, tempting him, that they might have to accuse him. But Jesus stooped down, and with his finger wrote on the ground, as though he heard them not. . . . When Jesus had lifted up himself, and saw none but the woman, he said unto her, Woman, where are those thine accusers? hath no man condemned thee? She said, No man, Lord. And Jesus said unto her, Neither do I condemn thee: go, and sin no more.

This is one of the most telling stories in any of the Gospel accounts. Two things strike me:

Jesus did not stand around posturing, attempting to look and act like Someone special. I have read that other authors feel he must have written something profound in the dirt at his feet. I doubt that. Of course, it wouldn't change anything for us if he did, but I think he was *doodling*. Much as one of us would doodle while waiting for some boring, dull tirade to end. He knew perfectly well that the scribes and Pharisees had brought the wretched adultress to him—not to make certain that her punishment was just, but to trap *him*. He knew everything the old boys were going to say, knew their tricky motives, knew their tired old logic. *Only the woman was important to him.* He knew *she* could be redeemed. They could not be as long as they stayed locked up in their precious *status quo*. He stooped down and doodled on the ground for a while, as though hoping they would go away. When they didn't, he straightened up and said something that would send them scurrying while there was time.

And then he used the whole incident redemptively. Not only to forgive the woman's sins, but to point up once more that the Son of God did not come to condemn. One thing that comes to me which I have never thought of before, is that *she* waited.

vv. 21, 22

> *Then said Jesus again unto them, I go my way, and ye shall seek me, and shall die in your sins: whither I go, ye cannot come. Then said the Jews, Will he kill himself? because he saith, Whither I go, ye cannot come.*

They were really in the dark. Mixed up! Does this give any hint of how important it is for us that Pentecost *has* happened?

v. 58

> *Jesus said unto them, Verily, verily, I say unto you, Before Abraham was, I am.*

"In the beginning was the Word, and the Word was with God, and the Word was God!" (The exclamation point is mine.)

CHAPTER 9

vv. 1 through 3

> *And as Jesus passed by, he saw a man which was blind from his birth. And his disciples asked him, saying, Master, who did sin, this man, or his parents, that he was born blind? Jesus answered, Neither hath this man*

sinned, nor his parents: but that the works of God should be made manifest in him.

Here is the old question which haunts so many shallow thinkers. Is extreme suffering—say blindness —caused by extreme sinning? Haven't you heard the "righteous" fortunate person click his or her tongue and declare: "Well, look how he lived. God is punishing him with this affliction!" Nonsense. Jesus does relate sin to suffering, but *not* in specifics like this. He said: "Neither hath this man sinned, nor his parents." God was about to be glorified in the healing. (Not only the healing of the man's eyes, as we shall see in the next passage, but his entire being.) Who had sinned and who hadn't is beside the point. Why do we insist upon generalizing everything Jesus said?

vv. 10, 11

Therefore said they unto him, How were thine eyes opened? He answered and said, A man that is called Jesus made clay, and anointed mine eyes, and said unto me, Go to the pool of Siloam, and wash: and I went and washed, and I received sight.

There begins an interesting *sequence of the birth of faith* here: In these two verses, we see the man who had been healed of his blindness giving Jesus the credit, but calling him merely: "A *man* that is called Jesus. . . ."

v. 17

They say unto the blind man again, What sayest thou of him, that he hath opened thine eyes? He said, He is a prophet.

He has progressed a step. He is now saying: "He is a *prophet.*"

vv. 24, 25

Then again called they the man that was blind, and said unto him, Give God the praise: we know that this man is a sinner. He answered and said, Whether he be a sinner or no, I know not: one thing I know, that, whereas I was blind, now I see.

They press him again and he witnesses strongly. He has taken a further step.

vv. 27 through 32

He answered them, I have told you already, and ye did not hear: wherefore would ye hear it again? will ye also be his disciples? Then they reviled him, and said, Thou art his disciple; but we are Moses' disciples. We know that God spake unto Moses: as for this fellow, we know not from whence he is. The man answered and said unto them, Why herein is a marvellous thing, that ye know not from whence he is, and yet he hath opened mine eyes. Now we know that God heareth not sinners: but if any man be a worshipper of God, and doeth his will, him he heareth. Since the world began was it not heard that any man opened the eyes of one that was born blind.

He witnesses again *and* preaches them quite a little sermon in the process. One can feel this young man's faith taking root!

vv. 33 through 38

If this man were not of God, he could do nothing. They answered and said unto him, Thou wast altogether born in sins, and dost thou teach us? And they cast him

*out. Jesus heard that they had cast him out; and when
he had found him, he said unto him, Dost thou believe
on the Son of God? He answered and said, Who is he,
Lord, that I might believe on him? And Jesus said unto
him, Thou hast both seen him, and it is he that talketh
with thee. And he said, Lord, I believe, And he worshipped him.*

When Jesus heard that the Pharisees had thrown the
harassed young man out, *Jesus went looking for him
and found him.* And the beautiful culmination of the
birth of the boy's faith comes with the *personal en-
counter* with Christ. As soon as he realized that God
loved him enough to seek him out personally, he believed. "And he worshipped him."

CHAPTER 10

vv. 1 through 5

*Verily, verily, I say unto you, He that entereth not by
the door into the sheepfold, but climbeth up some other
way, the same is a thief and a robber. But he that
entereth in by the door is the shepherd of the sheep.
To him the porter openeth; and the sheep hear his voice:
and he calleth his own sheep by name, and leadeth them
out. And when he putteth forth his own sheep, he goeth
before them, and the sheep follow him: for they know
his voice. And a stranger will they not follow, but will
flee from him: for they know not the voice of strangers.*

John recounts few parables. This one is very simple—the subject matter familiar to them all. It is
merely a description of a sheepfold, its door, its shep-

herd, and a statement of what they already knew: if anyone attempted to get at the sheep through any but the main door, which would always be opened for the shepherd, that person would be an intruder, possibly intent upon stealing the sheep. The Eastern shepherd, also, did not drive his sheep, he led them. He went "before." And no flock of sheep would follow a "shepherd" with a strange voice.

vv. 7 through 11

Then said Jesus unto them again, Verily, verily, I say unto you, I am the door of the sheep. All that ever came before me are thieves and robbers: but the sheep did not hear them. I am the door: by me if any man enter in, he shall be saved, and shall go in and out, and find pasture. The thief cometh not, but for to steal, and to kill, and to destroy: I am come that they might have life, and that they might have it more abundantly. I am the good shepherd: the good shepherd giveth his life for the sheep.

He is explaining to his disciples that he is not pointing them merely to the right door, that he *is the door*. He is the only possible way for a man to enter fully into relationship with the Father. Anyone who claims to be able to give life—new life—in any other name than the name of the crucified Saviour (who will lay down his very life for the sheep) is a thief or a robber. I do not at all think, as I have read elsewhere, that Jesus is saying that the Old Testament prophets were false prophets. They prophesied his coming. He refers to religious traditions other than the Judeo-Christian

here. He calls himself the "good shepherd," too, and I
doubt if any one of us has ever dwelt long enough on
that concept. Still, I am newly struck with his having
called himself "the door." "I am the door: by me if
any man enter in, he shall be saved, and shall go in and
out, and find pasture." Where I now live, I am more
aware of the necessity of going out. As long as I was
a city cliff-dweller, I went out when I had to, but
thought little of going out otherwise. Now, at almost
every "pause in the day's occupations," I go outside.
I see no rooftops, only vast stretches of wide marsh and
dense woods. My house is literally riddled with windows, so I can see outside even when I'm in. In the
geographical location of my house, I have found new
freedom. If *he* is the door, and if we can go in and out
by him, isn't he speaking of a new freedom here? Isn't
he holding out to us the potential of still more freedom
than most of us have conceived? The very freedom of
knowing that even when we are walking helplessly
into trouble or out of peace, he is still *the door?* And
the good shepherd?

vv. 14 through 16

*I am the good shepherd, and know my sheep, and am
known of mine. As the Father knoweth me, even so
know I the Father: and I lay down my life for the sheep.
And other sheep I have, which are not of this fold: them
also I must bring, and they shall hear my voice; and
there shall be one fold, and one shepherd.*

Mention the name of Jesus and watch the blank
looks on some faces. They evidently do not know his

voice. And of course, do not know he is *their* shepherd, too.

These blank looks don't follow the mention of God, only the name of Jesus Christ. It is like an embarrassment. This is no criticism of them—only of us who keep him a secret. Real relationship—adequate living—is the inevitable result when the shepherd who knows his sheep abides with the sheep who know their shepherd. It is as simple as that.

In verse 16, Jesus is not letting the disciples get by with their being exclusive. They tended to be, you know, as we do. The God of the New Testament is never, never exclusive. Always inclusive.

vv. 17 through 20

Therefore doth my Father love me, because I lay down my life, that I might take it again. No man taketh it from me, but I lay it down of myself. I have power to lay it down, and I have power to take it again. This commandment have I received of my Father. There was a division therefore again among the Jews for these sayings. And many of them said, He hath a devil, and is mad; why hear ye him?

He did not have to die, and he made that clear. He was pulling no punches now. The end was near. And the people thought he was mad! It seems strange to us, knowing that the Jews had been conditioned to the sacrifice for sins, that they did not catch his meaning. And yet I suppose it really isn't so strange. What he was about to do was so foreign to any concept man held of God, it must have been unbelievable. They had been

accustomed to making their own sacrifices before God
—it never occurred to them that God might make his
own *for sheer love of them.*

v. 23, 24, 30

> *And Jesus walked in the temple in Solomon's porch.
> Then came the Jews round about him, and said unto
> him, How long dost thou make us to doubt? If thou be
> the Christ, tell us plainly. . . . I and my Father are one.*

John here reaches another crescendo. The people
asked Jesus point-blank if he was the Christ, and he
answered them in a rising outburst of truth which cul-
minated in the one claim which drove his accusers to
a white-hot fury: "I and my Father are one." To claim
equality with the Lord God of Israel was to them the
ultimate blasphemy.

CHAPTER 11

vv. 5, 6

> *Now Jesus loved Martha, and her sister, and Lazarus.
> When he had heard therefore that he was sick, he abode
> two days still in the same place where he was.*

We miss much of the value of this poignant narrative if we don't have it straight that Mary and Martha
and Lazarus were close, personal friends of Jesus. In
recent months, they had become like chosen members
of his own family. From Luke's narrative, we know
something of the intimacy of Jesus' relationship with
the little family at Bethany. He loved them and he
knew them *as they were.* He knew Mary to be more

spiritually hungry than Martha, but he knew Martha to be more responsible in her daily round. Perhaps even fussy about it. He knew Lazarus as their young brother, eager to learn, the man of the family. Jesus was "at home" with the three. He went there often because he chose to. He liked to. He loved them. They could not be expected to understand a two-day delay. I have read and heard endless theories as to why Jesus waited. Somewhere in an earlier book, I may have had a few theories myself. Now, it seems unimportant for us to have a specific reason. Couldn't it have been that Jesus was merely waiting until he knew it was God's time? God was going to be glorified in the urgent meeting with Mary and Martha, and only Jesus would have known the appointed time. God was going to be glorified in the raising of Lazarus from the dead *and* in the Crucifixion of Jesus. Going back into Judea guaranteed that Crucifixion. He knew this. The family at Bethany was prominent. There would be no chance of keeping his visit a secret, even if he had wanted to. He was walking *now* steadily toward the Cross.

vv. 23 through 27

Jesus saith unto her, Thy brother shall rise again. Martha saith unto him, I know that he shall rise again in the resurrection at the last day. Jesus said unto her, I am the resurrection, and the life: he that believeth in me, though he were dead, yet shall he live: And whosoever liveth and believeth in me shall never die. Believest thou this? She saith unto him, Yea, Lord: I believe that thou art the Christ, the Son of God, which should come into the world.

Martha has run complaining to Jesus that if he had been there her brother would not have died. When he said: "Thy brother shall rise again," Martha answered, "Yes, yes, I know all about the resurrection on the last day, but—" Jesus stopped her with one of his most stunning claims: "I am the resurrection, and the life: he that believeth in me, though he were dead, yet shall he live: And whosoever liveth and believeth in me shall never die." Martha, up to that point, although she was a follower of Jesus, still clung comfortlessly to the old Pharisee doctrine of "the last day." She wasn't interested in "last days" now. She was concerned with today when her beloved brother lay dead in his grave. But then, Jesus must have looked at her, quieting her scattered, grief-stricken thoughts because when he asked her if *she* believed what he had said, the normally fussy, anxious woman replied unequivocally: "Yea, Lord: I believe that thou art the Christ, the Son of God, which should come into the world." Martha went further than he had asked her to go. Or perhaps she suddenly saw that believing that Jesus is *life*, is synonymous with believing that he is the Christ.

vv. 32 through 36

Then when Mary was come where Jesus was, and saw him, she fell down at his feet, saying unto him, Lord, if thou hadst been here, my brother had not died, When Jesus therefore saw her weeping, and the Jews also weep-

ing which came with her, he groaned in the spirit, and was troubled, And said, Where have ye laid him? They said unto him, Lord, come and see. Jesus wept. Then said the Jews, Behold how he loved him!

When Mary ran to meet Jesus, weeping, he was very different with her. He *knew* both sisters. With Mary, *he* wept too. And surely, it would be a mistake to eliminate human sorrow from verse 35: "Jesus wept." He loved Lazarus, too. He hated to think of the fine mind struck dumb by death, the once strong young body stiff and cold, beginning to decay in an airless tomb. He hated the grief he saw in the eyes of Lazarus' sisters. But I believe the storm of grief that tore through him, causing him to weep, was also his own soul trembling with hatred—*the holy hatred of God for anything that causes suffering among his children.* Every time he had performed a miracle during his earthly ministry, he must have struggled with all the dark powers that lay behind sin and death and destruction. He did not heal without cost to himself. When the woman with the "issue of blood" touched him—touched merely the hem of his garment—he felt virtue go out of him. It is as though some of this constant struggle were released here as he wept with Mary. He was on his way to Calvary to overcome these dark powers, but Calvary was not quite yet. And Jesus wept.

vv. 38 and 43

Jesus therefore again groaning in himself cometh to the grave. It was a cave, and a stone lay upon it. . . . And

when he thus had spoken, he cried with a loud voice,
Lazarus, come forth.

The great upheaval within Jesus kept him groaning
in himself as he walked with Mary to the place they
had buried Lazarus, his friend. After his prayer to the
Father for the people's sake, and for his own, he cried
with a loud voice: "Lazarus, come forth!" Jesus did
not need to shout in order to raise Lazarus. It has
meaning for me, at least, that his own human emotions
were climaxed in what he *knew* he was going to accom-
plish.

v. 44

And he that was dead came forth, bound hand and foot
with graveclothes: and his face was bound about with a
napkin. Jesus saith unto them. Loose him, and let him go.

God had raised Lazarus, but Jesus, always wanting
participation on our part, gave the people something
to do: "Loose him and let him go."

vv. 53, 54

Then from that day forth they took counsel together
for to put him to death. Jesus therefore walked no more
openly among the Jews; but went thence unto a country
near to the wilderness, into a city called Ephraim, and
there continued with his disciples.

The die was cast for certain now, after the raising
of Lazarus. The people were so impressed, his enemies
knew they had no choice but to be rid of him. And
Jesus "walked no more openly among the Jews"; but

went to Ephraim and spent time with his disciples, presumably still teaching and healing.

CHAPTER 12

vv. 1 through 3

Then Jesus six days before the passover came to Bethany, where Lazarus was which had been dead, whom he raised from the dead. There they made him a supper; and Martha served: but Lazarus was one of them that sat at the table with him. Then took Mary a pound of ointment of spikenard, very costly, and anointed the feet of Jesus, and wiped his feet with her hair: and the house was filled with the odour of the ointment.

Hatred toward him and love for him were at an all-time high. Actively, his death was being planned in Jerusalem. And his disciples were spending as much time with him as possible, some, like Mary, the sister of Lazarus, showing her adoration in every conceivable way. Lazarus sat at dinner with Jesus the night his sister, Mary, anointed her Lord with a pound of ointment of spikenard and wiped his feet with her hair. There is a variation here from the other Gospels, but whoever the woman was who anointed Jesus for his burial, the motive is the same—*love for him,* and that is what matters.

vv. 4 through 8

Then saith one of his disciples, Judas Iscariot, Simon's son, which should betray him, Why was not this ointment sold for three hundred pence, and given to the poor? This he said, not that he cared for the poor; but because he was a thief, and had the bag, and bare what was put therein. Then said Jesus, Let her alone: against the day of my burying hath she kept this. For the poor always ye have with you; but me ye have not always.

Judas Iscariot is tipping his hand. He does not care that much for the poor, or so John believed, but he is constantly exposing his impatient, materialistic nature. The nature that drove him to betray his Master for thirty pieces of silver. Jesus is not suggesting that it does not matter about the suffering of the poor. He is pointing out the difference between charity and adoration of God. One does not rule out the other, but the two are not to be passed off as the same. Both are essential.

vv. 12 through 16

On the next day much people that were come to the feast, when they heard that Jesus was coming to Jerusalem, Took branches of palm trees, and went forth to meet him, and cried, Hosanna: Blessed is the King of Israel that cometh in the name of the Lord. And Jesus, when he had found a young ass, sat thereon; as it is written, Fear not, daughter of Sion: behold, thy King cometh, sitting on an ass's colt. These things understood not his disciples at the first: but when Jesus was glorified, then remembered they that these things were written of him, and that they had done these things unto him.

Jesus' fame spread like wildfire after he raised Lazarus from the dead. It roared and crackled around his head wherever he went. And of course, when the people learned that he was coming to Jerusalem for the feast of the Passover, they cheered and threw flowers and shouted praises all along his route to the Holy City. His disciples did not understand why he insisted upon riding into Jerusalem on an ass's colt, but when he died, they realized it had been written of him. What a shocking time of realization those men had up ahead.

vv. 32, 33

And I, if I be lifted up from the earth, will draw all men unto me, This he said, signifying what death he should die.

The depths of meaning which lie here in this brief, certain statement of Jesus', we cannot possibly know. No one can know all he meant. We can know, however, that he said if he is lifted up, he will draw *all men* unto him. Does this sound as though the Lord God has picked out a select few? Was Jesus wrong? Dare we believe that he will draw all men unto him? My heart shouts yes! And yet, I know the violence that is unleashed among the saints of God who seem to expect a sparsely populated heaven. I know that "no man cometh unto the Father except by" Jesus Christ. What did he mean by saying "I, if I be lifted up from the earth, will draw *all men* unto me?" John inserts one of his explanatory notes in verse 33: "This he said, signifying what death he should die." And yet, if that was all Jesus meant, he could have merely said: "I am to be lifted up from the earth on a Cross." But he added that when this occurred, he would draw all men unto him. One thing I know: If his love is truly motivating our lives, *we long* for God to have a more far-reaching, vastly wider plan than he has felt it wise to reveal to us.

vv. 44 through 46

Jesus cried and said, He that believeth on me, believeth not on me, but on him that sent me. And he that seeth me seeth him that sent me. I am come a light into the world, that whosoever believeth on me should not abide in darkness.

His words speak for themselves here, but I am enlightened by the fact that John tells us "Jesus cried and said . . ." This is his last chance at the multitudes. His longing over them caused him to cry aloud one more time, in one more valiant effort to get through to them.

CHAPTER 13

v. 1

Now before the feast of the passover, when Jesus knew that his hour was come that he should depart out of this world unto the Father, having loved his own which were in the world, he loved them unto the end.

". . . he loved them unto the end." Rieu translates this: ". . . and now he showed how utterly he loved them."

vv. 3 through 5

Jesus knowing that the Father had given all things into his hands, and that he was come from God, and went to God; He riseth from supper, and laid aside his garments; and took a towel, and girded himself. After that he poureth water into a bason, and began to wash the disciples' feet, and to wipe them with the towel wherewith he was girded.

Jesus was secure in his own identity. He could perform this task, normally done by a slave, with perfect poise. Nothing *could* demean him. There is a great truth here for us: If we are secure in our identities as children of God, neither can we be insulted, belittled, demeaned.

v. 30

> *He then having received the sop went immediately out: and it was night.*

Judas could no longer stay in the presence of the One he had betrayed. I doubt that he was merely obeying his Master by leaving abruptly. It is true that Jesus had said: "That thou doest, do quickly." But Judas *had* to run. Out of the lighted room, out of the light of the Lord's presence—"and it was night" where he ran.

vv. 33 through 35

> *Little children, yet a little while I am with you. Ye shall seek me: and as I said unto the Jews, Whither I go, ye cannot come, so now I say to you. A new commandment I give unto you, That ye love one another; as I have loved you, that ye also love one another. By this shall all men know that ye are my disciples, if ye have love one to another.*

"Little children, yet a little while I am with you." For he loved them. The time was very short now to be together in the old, familiar, intimate way. And he reminded them that (as he had told the Jews), they, too, would seek him, but where he would be, they could not follow. For this reason, he must say to them what he felt to be the most important thing he had ever said: *They were to love each other as he had loved them!* This would be the way men would know that they were the disciples of Jesus Christ—if they truly loved each other. He did not say men would recognize them as Christians if they attended church every Sunday, if they tithed their money, if they studied the Scriptures, if they prayed. He said men would know *if they loved.* And they were to love each other. A cross on the steeple and a Christian name on the church sign do not make a church *Christian.* Men will know a church is a church made up of the followers of Jesus Christ only if they show love *toward each other.*

vv. 36 through 38

Simon Peter said unto him, Lord, whither goest thou? Jesus answered him, Whither I go, thou canst not follow me now; but thou shalt follow me afterwards. Peter said unto him, Lord, why cannot I follow thee now? I will lay down my life for thy sake. Jesus answered him, Wilt thou lay down thy life for my sake? Verily, verily, I say unto thee, The cock shall not crow, till thou hast denied me thrice.

Peter, like so many of us, was hung up on a technicality. He missed what Jesus had to say about love because he was curious to know where Jesus was going!

CHAPTER 14

vv. 1 through 4

Let not your heart be troubled: ye believe in God, believe also in me. In my Father's house are many

*mansions: if it were not so, I would have told you. I go to
prepare a place for you. And if I go and prepare a place
for you, I will come again, and receive you unto myself;
that where I am, there ye may be also. And whither I
go ye know, and the way ye know.*

Jesus did not humiliate Peter by ignoring his question (end of Chapter 13). Even after he warned the big
fisherman that he would deny him three times before
the cock crowed in the morning, he used Peter's question as a springboard for one of his most glorious statements. The disciples were not to let their hearts be
troubled because he was going away. They were to
trust him. "Do not be worried and upset." (*Good
News for Modern Man.*) "I am going to prepare a place
for you," he said, and added (I think importantly) that
if it were not so, *he* would have told them! I have,
through the years, formed the habit of adding this assurance to all the statements of Christ and it is enor-
mously strengthening and enlightening. For example:
"I and the Father are one. . . ." *If it were not so, I would
have told you.* "And I will pray the Father and he shall
give you another Comforter. . . ." *If it were not so, I
would have told you.* "I am the door. . . ." *If it were not
so, I would have told you.* "I am the good shepherd.
. . ." *If it were not so, I would have told you.* "Lo, I am
with you always." *If it were not so, I would have told
you.* He is trustworthy. And he was on his way that
night to prepare a place for them in his Father's house.
For each one of them. If it were not so, he would *have
told them.*

vv. 5 through 7

Thomas saith unto him, Lord, we know not whither thou goest; and how can we know the way? Jesus saith unto him, I am the way, the truth, and the life: no man cometh unto the Father, but by me. If ye had known me, ye should have known my Father also: and from henceforth ye know him, and have seen him.

Perhaps their fear of losing him muddied their memories. At least Thomas asked point blank: "Lord, we know not whither thou goest; and how can we know the way?" Jesus, once more, used an obvious, panic-induced question to point up a central truth: "I am the way, Thomas. I am the way. I am the truth. I am the whole of life!" (My own interpolation.) In other words, anyone can know the way by knowing the One who himself *is* the way. And I am forever grateful that he clarified further that he had come to make the Father plain: "If ye had known me, ye should have known my Father also: and from henceforth ye know him, and have seen him." Anyone who has seen Jesus Christ has a definite idea of what God is really like. It is unavoidable.

vv. 8 through 11

Philip saith unto him, Lord, shew us the Father, and it sufficeth us. Jesus saith unto him, Have I been so long time with you, and yet hast thou not known me, Philip? he that hath seen me hath seen the Father; and how sayest thou then, Shew us the Father? Believest thou not that I am in the Father, and the Father in me? the words that

I speak unto you I speak not of myself: but the Father that dwelleth in me, he doeth the works. Believe me that I am in the Father, and the Father in me: or else believe me for the very works' sake.

John does a remarkable writing job here in helping us once more through his remembered dialogue between Philip and the Master. After Jesus' explanation to Thomas, it seems impossible that anyone could still have a question concerning the Father. And yet we do, as Philip did, and John, bless him, has further clarified.

v. 14

If ye shall ask any thing in my name, I will do it.

Add to this promise: "If it were not so, I would have told you," and you will find it easier to act upon and to believe.

vv. 16 through 18

And I will pray the Father, and he shall give you another Comforter, that he may abide with you for ever; Even the Spirit of truth; whom the world cannot receive, because it seeth him not, neither knoweth him: but ye know him; for he dwelleth with you, and shall be in you. I will not leave you comfortless: I will come to you.

Jesus promises them that God will send the Comforter, the Holy Spirit of God himself. He did not merely say "The Father will send you some form of comfort." He said *Someone* was coming! And then, to me *most meaningfully*, in almost the same breath, Jesus said: "I will come to you." The Holy Spirit, when he came, would not be a stranger to them. Jesus and the Father and the Holy Spirit are *one*. When the Spirit would come to live with and within the disciples, they would no longer be grieving and lonely and lost. I dare to believe that what Jesus was saying was that the same Spirit which they had seen in him, to which they had been so attracted, would then be with them forever. In a definite sense, he himself would be coming back to them. "I will come to you." The Book of Acts tells the story of his first return.

vv. 25, 26

These things have I spoken unto you, being yet present with you. But the Comforter, which is the Holy Ghost, whom the Father will send in my name, he shall teach you all things, and bring all things to your remembrance, whatsoever I have said unto you.

He was doing all he could to make things clear to them on their last night together, but he well knew they were getting almost none of it. Even to this, he said in effect: "Don't worry if you do not grasp all I say. This same coming Comforter will teach you what you need to know and bring it to mind for you when you need it." (My interpolation.)

CHAPTER 15

vv. 1 through 5

I am the true vine, and my Father is the husbandman. Every branch in me that beareth not fruit he taketh away: and every branch that beareth fruit, he purgeth it, that it may bring forth more fruit. Now ye are clean through the word which I have spoken unto you. Abide

*in me, and I in you. As the branch cannot bear fruit of
itself, except it abide in the vine; no more can ye, except
ye abide in me. I am the vine, ye are the branches: He
that abideth in me, and I in him, the same bringeth forth
much fruit: for without me ye can do nothing.*

I see this now, almost twenty years after my own
conversion to Jesus Christ, as the simplest possible
teaching concerning the tremendous potential of pro-
ductivity and rest available to us through the indwell-
ing Holy Spirit. Did you ever hear of a branch *pleading* with its vine to send down more sap so that it could
live and bear fruit? The branch merely stays on the
vine—and *expects*.

vv. 8, 9

*Herein is my Father glorified, that ye bear much fruit;
so shall ye be my disciples. As the Father hath loved me,
so have I loved you: continue ye in my love.*

Jesus said God, his Father, was glorified *if* his disciples bear much fruit. How have we so distorted this
as to mean that the Father is only glorified according
to how many "souls we win?" I have never won a soul
to Christ. None of us has. God does his own winning
and the sooner we learn this the more rested and re-
laxed and natural we are going to be as children in the
Kingdom. Jesus said, don't forget, that if he were lifted
up he would do his own drawing. The fruit that glor-
ifies the Father has been listed for us by Paul (Gala-
tians 5:22). And soul winning is *not* on the list. These
characteristics of Christ himself, *are* on the list: "Love,

joy, peace, patience, kindness, generosity, fidelity, tolerance and self-control" (Phillips). Love heads the list! And as Jesus said: "Continue ye in my love."

v. 14

Ye are my friends, if ye do whatsoever I command you.

Jesus was not merely being strict. Doing what he commands has nothing whatever to do with love *unless* we are obeying because we believe with all our beings that *he knows best.* Duty is not the point at all.

v. 15

Henceforth I call you not servants; for the servant knoweth not what his lord doeth: but I have called you friends; for all things that I have heard of my Father I have made known unto you.

When people write and preach about the necessity of *serving* the Lord, I wonder if they have forgotten what Jesus said that last night: ". . . the servant knoweth not what his lord doeth: but I have called you friends; for all things that I have heard of my Father I have made known unto you." A servant serves his master blindly. We are not living in the dark! Jesus Christ has chosen us to be his *friends.* It is far simpler to be a servant than a friend. I never think of how well or how poorly I am "serving" the Lord. I don't think in terms of service at all. Rather, *am I his friend?* Friends share. Friends make each other glad or sad or hopeful or hopeless. Friends support each other. Friends love. Do I love him? Do you? Friendship has to do with *being*. Service can be mere *doing*.

vv. 26, 27

> *But when the Comforter is come, whom I will send unto you from the Father, even the Spirit of truth, which proceedeth from the Father, he shall testify of me: And ye also shall bear witness, because ye have been with me from the beginning.*

Once more, he promises that they will understand his meaning *after* the Comforter comes to them. They will feel at home with the Holy Spirit because he will testify to them of Jesus. They will feel familiar with him because they will be reminded of the very essence of the personality of their Master whom they loved so dearly. And they will bear witness to their comfort and peace with the Spirit, because they have been with Jesus from the beginning. In other words, the world will know they are *still* with Jesus! Their grief gone, their spirits elevated, their minds cleared, their courage high, their love strong.

CHAPTER 16

vv. 5 through 14, 20, 22

> *But now I go my way to him that sent me; and none of you asketh me, Whither goest thou? But because I have said these things unto you, sorrow hath filled your heart. Nevertheless I tell you the truth; It is expedient for you that I go away: for if I go not away, the Comforter will not come unto you; but if I depart, I will send him unto you. And when he is come, he will reprove the world of*

sin, and of righteousness, and of judgment: Of sin, because they believe not on me; Of righteousness, because I go to my Father, and ye see me no more; Of judgment, because the prince of this world is judged. I have yet many things to say unto you, but ye cannot bear them now. Howbeit when he, the Spirit of truth, is come, he will guide you into all truth: for he shall not speak of himself; but whatsoever he shall hear, that shall he speak: and he will shew you things to come. He shall glorify me: for he shall receive of mine, and shall shew it unto you. . . . and ye shall be sorrowful, but your sorrow shall be turned into joy. . . . I will see you again, and your heart shall rejoice, and your joy no man taketh from you.

He has given them the assurance of the Holy Spirit, but they are still blinded by their sorrow at losing him. (Of all people on earth, Jesus understands grief.) He tries reasoning with them, to show them that it will be far better for them if he returns to his Father, *so that* the Spirit may come to them. I imagine he "lost" them as he attempted to explain all the Spirit would do, but in verse 20, he found a response again when he said: ". . . ye shall be sorrowful, but your sorrow shall be turned to joy." They could take his word for things; this they knew. I feel, at least, that had I been one of the disciples that night, I should have clung to the fact that he said my sorrow would somehow be turned to joy. "I will see you again, and your heart shall rejoice, and your joy no man taketh from you." The grief remains, but the sting is gone from death when we can really believe that "I will see you again."

v. 33

These things I have spoken unto you, that in me ye might have peace. In the world ye shall have tribulation: but be of good cheer; I have overcome the world.

He was always realistic with them. He is always realistic with us. Life is not going to be easy. There will be plenty of trouble ahead. No man is immune. But, the Lord said we were to "be of good cheer [because] I have overcome the world." He does not imply that he will see that everyone is kind to us, or that he will fill our storehouses with wealth. He said these things so we "might have peace" *in the midst of* tribulations, knowing nothing can ever change him. In this way, if our eye is single—filled with Jesus only—we can never be overcome because he has overcome the downpull of the world and we are *free in him.* "If the Son . . . shall make you free, ye shall be free indeed" (John 8:36).

CHAPTER 17

v. 3

And this is life eternal, that they might know thee the only true God, and Jesus Christ, whom thou hast sent.

Jesus gives eternal life because it is only through him that anyone can really know what God is like: *can know God.* And Jesus' own definition of eternal life is —*to know God.*

v. 4

> *I have glorified thee on the earth: I have finished the work which thou gavest me to do.*

Nothing remained at this point, but the supreme revelation of God's own heart on the Cross. The Lamb had been slain before the foundation of the world. Jesus did not *change* the Father's heart toward us as he hung there. He was revealing it—supremely.

v. 5

> *And now, O Father, glorify thou me with thine own self with the glory which I had with thee before the world was.*

We cannot know all of what he means here, but surely, he is saying in part, at least: "Oh, Father, now let me come home!"

vv. 6 through 11

> *I have manifested thy name unto the men which thou gavest me out of the world: thine they were, and thou gavest them me; and they have kept thy word. Now they have known that all things whatsoever thou hast given me are of thee. For I have given unto them the words which thou gavest me; and they have received them, and have known surely that I came out from thee, and they have believed that thou didst send me. I pray for them: I pray not for the world, but for them which thou hast given me; for they are thine. And all mine are thine, and thine are mine; and I am glorified in them. And now I am no more in the world, but these are in the world, and I come to thee. Holy Father, keep through*

thine own name those whom thou hast given me, that
they may be one, as we are.

How sensitive of Jesus to permit his disciples to hear
his own special prayer for them! This is one of life's
truly encouraging and comforting experiences, to be
permitted to hear someone pray for us. I do not think
Jesus was refusing in any way to petition the Father
in behalf of those who were still not believers when he
said: "I pray not for the world. . . ." This was a particular time of fellowship and prayer with and for his
disciples—his chosen ones. Would the Man who poured
out his entire life for the multitudes refuse to pray for
them? This interpretation is superficial in the extreme.
He just wanted his men to know that *this prayer* was
especially for *them*.

v. 15

I pray not that thou shouldest take them out of the
world, but that thou shouldest keep them from the evil.

He didn't want them to shut themselves away to
lives of "holy contemplation." He wanted them "in the
world" where the need was, but showing that their own
needs had been met in him.

v. 18

As thou hast sent me into the world, even so have I
also sent them into the world.

In fact, he is *sending* them into the world. He did not
stay in glory, remote from man's sin and suffering, so

of course, he did not want his followers to seclude themselves with their own "spiritual experiences."

vv. 20 through 23

Neither pray I for these alone, but for them also which shall believe on me through their word; That they all may be one; as thou, Father, art in me, and I in thee, that they also may be one in us: that the world may believe that thou hast sent me. And the glory which thou gavest me I have given them; that they may be one, even as we are one: I in them, and thou in me, that they may be made perfect in one; and that the world may know that thou hast sent me, and hast loved them, as thou hast loved me.

He prayed for us too that night.

v. 24

Father, I will that they also, whom thou hast given me, be with me where I am; that they may behold my glory, which thou hast given me: for thou lovedst me before the foundation of the world.

And he prayed to be with his disciples and with us, Just think: He wants to be with *us*.

CHAPTER 18

vv. 1 through 3

When Jesus had spoken these words, he went forth with his disciples over the brook Cedron, where was a garden, into the which he entered, and his disciples. And Judas also, which betrayed him, knew the place: for Jesus ofttimes resorted thither with his disciples. Judas then, having received a band of men and officers

from the chief priests and Pharisees, cometh thither with
lanterns and torches and weapons.

The familiar spot in the garden "over the brook
Cedron," where Jesus and his disciples had gone together so often, was, on this night, eerie with long,
jumping shadows from the torches and lanterns carried
by the band of approaching soldiers. There was the
clank and rattle of swords and armor and the thud of
boots as the heavily armed company closed in on the
quiet Galilean. The restful, joy-filled, stimulating hours
they had known there in the better days were gone;
none of his men laughed now: they cowered in fright
and anger.

v. 4

Jesus therefore, knowing all things that should come
upon him, went forth, and said unto them, Whom seek
ye?

Jesus stepped quickly forward, poised, in full command of the situation—the really ludicrous situation.
"Whom seek ye?" he asked before one of his enemies
could collect himself enough to speak.

vv. 5, 6

They answered him, Jesus of Nazareth. Jesus saith
unto them, I am he. And Judas also, which betrayed
him, stood with them. As soon then as he had said unto
them, I am he, they went backward, and fell to the
ground.

Finally someone said that they sought Jesus of Nazareth. And when Jesus answered simply: "I am he," they all (presumably Judas, too,) fell back, surely in awe of both His commanding presence and His courage. Some of them even fell to the ground.

vv. 7, 8

Then asked he them again, Whom seek ye? And they said, Jesus of Nazareth. Jesus answered, I have told you that I am he: if therefore ye seek me, let these go their way:

Even here, Jesus was offering himself in his disciples' stead. "Take me. Let them go free." (My own interpolation.)

vv. 10, 11

Then Simon Peter having a sword drew it, and smote the high priest's servant, and cut off his right ear. The servant's name was Malchus. Then said Jesus unto Peter, Put up thy sword into the sheath: the cup which my Father hath given me, shall I not drink it?

Peter, in his outrage, drew his sword and cut off one man's ear. With the same authority and for the same basic reason, he once said: "Get thee behind me, Satan!" Jesus admonished him again: "Put up thy sword into the sheath: the cup which my Father hath given me, shall I not drink it?"

John does not describe Gethsemane, but this is its victory: ". . . shall I not drink it?"

v. 28

Then led they Jesus from Caiaphas unto the hall of judgment: and it was early; and they themselves went

not into the judgment hall, lest they should be defiled;
but that they might eat the passover.

The self-righteous Jews led Jesus first to Annas, the
father-in-law of the high priest, Caiaphas, but they
would not lead him into the judgment hall of the gen-
tile, Pilate, for fear of contaminating themselves so they
could not eat the Passover Feast. God pity their blindness, and through his Son, he did.

vv. 37, 38

Pilate therefore said unto him, Art thou a king then?
Jesus answered, Thou sayest that I am a king. To this
end was I born, and for this cause came I into the world,
that I should bear witness unto the truth. Every one
that is of the truth heareth my voice Pilate saith unto
him, What is truth? And when he had said this, he went
out again unto the Jews, and saith unto them, I find in
him no fault at all.

Jesus proclaimed truth to the pagan governor, Pilate,
and it appears that, for a fleeting moment, Pilate
thought. "What is truth?" he asked. But before Jesus
could answer, the expedient Pilate stopped thinking,
turned abruptly and went back outside to the Jews.

CHAPTER 19
v. 5

Then came Jesus forth, wearing the crown of thorns,
and the purple robe. And Pilate saith unto them, Behold
the man!

"Then came Jesus forth wearing the crown of thorns,
and the purple robe." Beaten, spat upon, bruised, blood

trickling from his head over his face. And Pilate said: "Behold the man!" Coming from Pilate, this could have meant: "Look here, this is the battered, helpless creature you would crucify! This is the bruised, harmless man you are afraid of!" John, however, seems to want to read into Pilate's words a deeper truth. He makes no explanation here, but his phrasing indicates it to me. And who knows that Pilate did not speak from the conflict in his own soul? After all, he had been with Jesus!

vv. 21, 22

Then said the chief priests of the Jews to Pilate, Write not, The King of the Jews; but that he said, I am King of the Jews. Pilate answered, What I have written I have written.

Is Pilate here unconsciously testifying to the truth?

vv. 26, 27

When Jesus therefore saw his mother, and the disciple standing by, whom he loved, he saith unto his mother, Woman, behold thy son! Then saith he to the disciple, Behold thy mother! And from that hour that disciple took her unto his own home.

The Son of God was *demonstrating* the very *heart* of his Father on the Cross—his arms stretched wide to embrace the whole world of lost men and women. But he took note of individual human need even as he suffered for all mankind: He gave his mother to his beloved disciple, John, and he gave John to his mother.

v. 30

When Jesus therefore had received the vinegar, he said, It is finished: and he bowed his head, and gave up the ghost.

This was not the end. This was the completion of the demonstration of God's heart—*as it really is.* Nothing could be added. And the demonstration was there for every man to see and to believe. Jesus was free at last to die, and he did, so that we might live.

vv. 32 through 37

Then came the soldiers, and brake the legs of the first, and of the other which was crucified with him. But when they came to Jesus, and saw that he was dead already, they brake not his legs: But one of the soldiers with a spear pierced his side, and forthwith came there out blood and water. And he that saw it bare record, and his record is true: and he knoweth that he saith true, that ye might believe. For these things were done, that the scripture should be fulfilled, A bone of him shall not be broken. And again another scripture saith, They shall look on him whom they pierced.

Dear John, writing his story of Jesus, remains to the end, so eager, so hopeful "that ye might believe."

CHAPTER 20

vv. 10 through 14

Then the disciples went away again unto their own home. But Mary stood without at the sepulchre weeping: and as she wept, she stooped down, and looked into the sepulchre, And seeth two angels in white sitting, the one

*at the head, and the other at the feet, where the body of
Jesus had lain. And they say unto her, Woman, why
weepest thou? She saith unto them, Because they have
taken away my Lord, and I know not where they have
laid him. And when she had thus said, she turned herself
back, and saw Jesus standing, and knew not that it was
Jesus.*

Mary of Magdala was, according to John's Gospel account, the first one there on that first day of the week
—"when it was yet dark." She could not stay away even
from the place where they had laid him, so great was
her grief, so great was her love. It was she who ran to
tell Peter and John that the tomb was empty, the stone
rolled away. Both men came running, examined the
visible evidence, found the empty sepulcher, the
folded-up grave cloths, "believed" at least, that Jesus
was not there, but evidently just turned around and
went home. Not Mary. Mary stood outside the empty
tomb, weeping, and once more stooped down and
looked inside. Her perseverance and her determination and her love were rewarded: Two angels asked her
why she wept. Her answer is the profoundly simple
reply of a woman with a broken heart: "I'm weeping,"
she said, "because they have taken away my Lord, and
I don't know where they have laid him." (My interpolation.) Still no one suspected he was not dead. Even
Mary's grief was unbroken. Was still unbroken, when
she turned and saw him standing beside her, because
she did not recognize him. She was there, for love of
him, but her *grief* had her attention.

vv. 15, 16

*Jesus saith unto her, Woman, why weepest thou?
whom seekest thou? She, supposing him to be the
gardener, saith unto him, Sir, if thou have borne him
hence, tell me where thou hast laid him, and I will take
him away. Jesus saith unto her, Mary. She turned herself,
and saith unto him, Rabboni; which is to say, Master.*

She wanted only his body, so that she could "take
him away" and care for him. Her sights were no higher
than that. And she still did not recognize him until he
spoke her name, "Mary." No one else had ever spoken
her name as he did.

v. 18

*Mary Magdalene came and told the disciples that she
had seen the Lord, and that he had spoken these things
unto her.*

Once more Mary ran to tell the disciples that she had
seen him! That he had spoken to her. There is no evidence that they believed her this time either.

vv. 19, 20

*Then the same day at evening, being the first day of
the week, when the doors were shut where the disciples
were assembled for fear of the Jews, came Jesus and stood
in the midst, and saith unto them, Peace be unto you.
And when he had so said, he shewed unto them his hands
and his side. Then were the disciples glad, when they
saw the Lord.*

Jesus knew they were locked up in a room, filled
with fears and anxieties and confusion. He also knew

they hadn't believed Mary or any of the women who had told them their Lord was risen. He knew this, and so he did what he had to do: he came to them personally, showing his hands and his pierced side, saying: "Peace to you. . . ." (He has come to me, as I write this, because he understands why I am confused and bewildered over a certain set of circumstances in my life right now. He has come, reminding me of his hands and his pierced side and he has *brought peace with him* —as he always does.)

vv. 24 through 28

But Thomas, one of the twelve, called Didymus, was not with them when Jesus came. The other disciples therefore said unto him, We have seen the Lord. But he said unto them, Except I shall see in his hands the print of the nails, and put my finger into the print of the nails, and thrust my hand into his side, I will not believe. And after eight days again his disciples were within, and Thomas with them: then came Jesus, the doors being shut, and stood in the midst, and said, Peace be unto you. Then saith he to Thomas, Reach hither thy finger, and behold my hands; and reach hither thy hand, and thrust it into my side: and be not faithless, but believing. And Thomas answered and said unto him, My Lord and my God.

Thomas happened not to be in the tightly barred room with the other disciples when Jesus came the first time, bringing his peace and assurance that all was well. And knowing Thomas, as only Jesus knew him, he came again—*just for Thomas*, the man with the inquiring, doubting mind. The man Jesus knew needed personal attention in order to quiet his doubts. Jesus always comes according to *our* needs. And he always comes according to our *realistic* needs, not our imagined ones. Thomas was not a weak soul. Jesus knew this. He simply had the kind of mind that demands logical answers. Once Thomas saw for himself, he fell to his knees saying: "My Lord and my God!" Jesus had not expected Thomas to accept a secondhand theological premise, a broad generality. Thomas needed a personal Lord, and a personal God and Jesus came in person—the second time, *just for Thomas.* The Master has not changed in these almost two thousand years.

v. 29

Jesus saith unto him, Thomas, because thou hast seen me, thou hast believed: blessed are they that have not seen, and yet have believed.

He was thinking of us too, even then. I do not feel he was belittling Thomas at all.

vv. 30, 31

And many other signs truly did Jesus in the presence of his disciples, which are not written in this book: But these are written, that ye might believe that Jesus is the Christ, the Son of God; and that believing ye might have life through his name.

John is again assuring and reassuring us—this time that there were many more signs of Jesus' resurrection, not recorded. I realize it is considered better literary form to remain objective. But when one is writing about the Lord God himself, it becomes urgent at times, to add a personal word. A witness. A firsthand testimony to what one knows from having experienced or from having seen with one's own eyes. John's eagerness that *we* find it possible to believe touches me.

CHAPTER 21

vv. 7, 8

Therefore that disciple whom Jesus loved saith unto Peter, It is the Lord. Now when Simon Peter heard that it was the Lord, he girt his fisher's coat unto him, (for he was naked,) and did cast himself into the sea. And the other disciples came in a little ship; (for they were not far from land, but as it were two hundred cubits,) dragging the net with fishes.

The men went back to Galilee, as he instructed. (John calls it the Sea of Tiberias since he was writing for Jewish readers. It is the same as the Sea of Galilee, where they had spent so many good hours with Jesus.) They were waiting for him to come to them, as he said he would. And being restless outdoor men, they grew fidgety. Finally, Peter said he was going fishing, and the others decided they'd go along. As on another night, before they crucified Jesus, the men caught nothing (Luke 5:5). And just at dawn, the Lord himself stood on the shore and asked them if they'd had any luck. None of the men recognized him, even when he called:

"Cast the net on the right side of the ship and ye shall find!" Being Jesus, understanding them all as he did, he chose this time to come to them. It was a familiar scene. Almost literally, it had all happened before. Still, they were blind to who he really was standing there shouting instructions to them over the misty waters. When they cast their nets on the right side, they were suddenly so heavy with fish it was more than the men could manage to draw back over the side of the boat! Then it dawned on John, the beloved disciple, that this had all happened before. He peered across the expanse of water and cried: "It is the Lord!" Peter, impetuous as ever, jumped overboard and began to swim toward his Master. The others followed quickly in the ship, with their enormous load of fish. Jesus did not meet them after his resurrection in an overwhelming majestic circumstance. He came to them in a situation where he knew *they* would feel at home.

vv. 9 through 13

As soon then as they were come to land, they saw a fire of coals there, and fish laid thereon, and bread. Jesus saith unto them, Bring of the fish which ye have now caught. Simon Peter went up, and drew the net to land full of great fishes, an hundred and fifty and three: and for all there were so many, yet was not the net broken. Jesus saith unto them, Come and dine. And none of the disciples durst ask him, Who art thou? knowing that it was the Lord. Jesus then cometh, and taketh bread, and giveth them, and fish likewise.

He was not only waiting for them on the shore, he had a fire built, bread ready and with the fish they had caught, *he cooked their breakfast for them.* "Come and dine!" "Breakfast's ready!"

v. 17

> *He saith unto him the third time, Simon, son of Jonas, lovest thou me? Peter was grieved because he said unto him the third time, Lovest thou me? And he said unto him, Lord, thou knowest all things; thou knowest that I love thee. Jesus saith unto him, Feed my sheep.*

It is helpful here to know the J. B. Phillips translation of this provocative and sometimes confusing passage:

"When they had finished breakfast Jesus said to Simon Peter, 'Simon, son of John, do you love me more than these others?'

" 'Yes, Lord,' he replied. 'You know that I am your friend.'

" 'Then feed my lambs,' returned Jesus. Then he said for the second time,

" 'Simon, son of John, do you love me?'

" 'Yes, Lord,' returned Peter. 'You know that I am your friend.'

" 'Then care for my sheep,' replied Jesus. Then for the third time, Jesus spoke to him and said,

" 'Simon, son of John, *are* you my friend?'

"Peter was deeply hurt because Jesus' third question to him was 'Are you my friend?' and he said: Lord, you know everything. You know that I am your friend!'

" 'Then feed my sheep,' Jesus said to him."

It seems important to me that Jesus did not call him Peter, the new name he had given him. The rock. After all, Peter had not acted like a rock during Jesus' passion and suffering. He had reverted to form—he had acted like Simon, the son of John. Not Peter, the son of God. I am also interested in the fact that Jesus kept asking Peter (using the word for love that denotes friendship) if he was really his *friend*. He did not ask him if he was his *servant*. Jesus was not starting at the wrong place. If Peter was going to be his true friend, then he would automatically "feed the sheep and the lambs." He would serve *naturally*. Friends do this. True friends always rejoice in serving each other. The sequence of questioning which Jesus used springs from divine wisdom. Divine wisdom is startlingly practical and always realistic.

Another thing that strikes me is that Jesus *kept asking*. Giving Peter ample time to see the point. That Peter didn't, that he only got his feelings hurt, should give us plenty of grounds for identification with the big disciple.

vv. 18, 19

Verily, verily, I say unto thee, When thou wast young, thou girdedst thyself, and walkedst whither thou wouldest: but when thou shalt be old, thou shalt stretch forth thy hands, and another shall gird thee, and carry thee whither thou wouldest not. This spake he, signifying by what death he should glorify God. And, when he had spoken this, he saith unto him, Follow me.

Jesus knew what lay up ahead for Peter: They were going to crucify him, too, as they had crucified his Lord. And Jesus was lovingly warning him—emphasizing once more the cost of discipleship. Because after he had told Peter of his death, he said: "Follow me." In other words, "Up ahead is trouble, my child, but follow me anyway."

vv. 20 through 22

> *Then Peter, turning about, seeth the disciple whom Jesus loved following; which also leaned on his breast at supper, and said, Lord, which is he that betrayeth thee? Peter seeing him saith to Jesus, Lord, and what shall this man do? Jesus saith unto him, If I will that he tarry till I come, what is that to thee? follow thou me.*

Peter looked around and saw John, the beloved disciple, nearby. And being Peter, he wanted to know what John's end would be. To the very close of John's Gospel, we have the chance to learn the meaning, the cost of true discipleship: Jesus said to Peter, in effect, that if John lived forever, that would be nothing to Peter. In short, none of his business. That would be strictly the business of God. Just as Jesus knew Peter *as Peter really was inside*, knew him to be *unlike any other man*, so Peter would have to settle (as do we all) for a unique walk with God. I do not see Jesus as critical of Peter here. He is *clarifying*. God's plan for one of us is not necessarily his plan for anyone else. Peter was merely to follow Jesus as he had during the earthly ministry—no matter where he led him. John, also, was to follow Jesus, no matter where he led.

v. 23

Then went this saying abroad among the brethren, that that disciple should not die: yet Jesus said not unto him, He shall not die; but, If I will that he tarry till I come, what is that to thee?

John ends the incident with a touch of wry humor. The gossips among the disciples were hard at it then, as they are hard at it now. "Then went this saying abroad" that John was not going to die! No doubt it was partly jealousy, because John and Jesus had been humanly very close. Whatever caused it, the end result was humor. It was plain old gossip. Thank heaven, Jesus died for the "plain old gossips," too.

vv. 24, 25

This is the disciple which testifieth of these things, and wrote these things: and we know that his testimony is true. And there are also many other things which Jesus did, the which, if they should be written every one, I suppose that even the world itself could not contain the books that should be written. Amen.

Once more, at the very close of his account, John is reaching a hand toward us to strengthen our faith. It may be true, as some scholars believe, that John, the beloved disciple, did not write this Gospel. But he seems to me to say here: "I, the disciple Jesus loved, am the witness to these things and I wrote them down." Either way, it is all right. John is not the central issue.

Jesus is. And along with his beloved friend, John, I too, "suppose that even the world itself could not contain the books that should be written" about the life and love and wonderful deeds of this Jesus Christ, the God we follow.